NO NEED TO GO NUTS

60 NUT-FREE RECIPES FOR ENJOYING FOOD AND LIFE WITH ALLERGIES

VICTORIA ZOLLA

DEDICATION

To the food allergy community for reminding me I am not alone in my struggles, advocating for our needs, creating valuable changes, and continuing the conversations that help the millions of people impacted by food allergies.

To healthcare professionals, first responders, researchers, allergy conscious chefs, and the business owners of allergy-safe snack brands, restaurants, and food technologies. For your work saves so many lives, helps keep those with food allergies safe, brings joy and hope, and has more of an impact than you may ever know. Thank you.

And to my family and close friends, for teaching me valuable lessons, supporting me through hard times, encouraging me to pursue my dreams, testing my recipes, and reminding me that I can do anything.

DISCLAIMER

While I have managed severe peanut and tree nut allergies since the age of four, and I have learned a lot about managing food allergies and nutrition through my own experiences, appointments, schooling, and research, I am not an expert. This cookbook is intended to be educational and informative, but it does not qualify as medical or professional advice and as such should be considered a supplementary resource. Please follow the guidance of your allergist, primary care doctor, dietitian and other experts in your life when making choices about food and your health. Allergy management, severity, and nutritional needs vary, and it is important to always keep this in mind.

Introduction	1
About the Author	3
Nut-Free Nutrition	6
Foods to Include	7
Breakfast	8
Lunch	30
Dinner	50
Snack	73
Dessert	88
Extra Eats	108
Additional Resources	124
Cooking Tips	126
Grocery Store Guidance	129
Acknowledgements	133
The Final Words	135

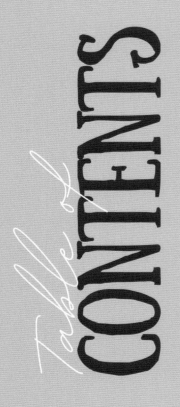

INTRODUCTION

While clever names and eye-catching photos lure me to open various cookbooks and visit different blogs when on the hunt for new recipes, it is usually only a matter of seconds before the book goes back on the shelf, or I hit the back arrow feeling defeated. No, I am not a picky eater, or too good to learn from someone else. This habitual loop of excitement and frustration is due to my life-threatening peanut and tree nut allergies that can make finding safe recipes a challenge and tiring act. Because nuts are important in various cuisines and prioritized due to their robust nutrient profiles, it is common to find cookbooks and web pages loaded with nut-containing recipes. Sure, I could just leave them out or find a different book, but what is the fun in that, and who has the time to scour the shelves of their local Barnes & Noble or the depths of the World Wide Web? Not me, and probably not you either if you are a busy student or young professional with a severe nut allergy.

Whether you are cooking for yourself for the first time, wondering what your options are, wanting some nutrient dense recipes, or hoping to add some new foods to an overused meal rotation, this book was made for you. This book aims to fill some gaps in the food space and potential nutritional gaps in your diet by providing you with various peanut and tree nut-free recipes for all meals of the day to help you consume the many nutrients commonly found in nuts and enjoy eating.

Although these recipes are organized by mealtime for convenience, they can be enjoyed whenever you desire. Sometimes our everyday stressors or self-doubt can make the idea of preparing an extensive meal intimidating, or our own body tells us that French toast or an omelet sounds like a better way to end the day than chicken, rice, and vegetables. That said, I encourage you to enjoy these nut-free recipes at any time you please.

NO NEED TO GO NUTS

No Need to Go Nuts was inspired by my own experiences navigating independent living as a peanut/tree nut-free girl and my curiosities about nutrition for those with and without food allergies. My first thought of wanting to write a cookbook came about after I graduated high school, but I did not feel qualified as an amateur who cooks and bakes as a hobby. I did not think I had the time nor the skills as I would be starting college. I thought maybe I would make one down the road to preserve family recipes, but I put this idea back on my bucket list and carried on. Looking back on it now, I am reminded of the value of patience and think that maybe this is one of those everything-happens-for-a-reason moments. Had I not gone to UMass, encountered these roadblocks that tested me, switched my major, and talked to friends and family members about my aspirations at length (thanks for listening by the way), I am not sure this project would have come to fruition.

I hope this compilation of recipes can help other young adults like me improve their eating habits and find joy in cooking and eating because I believe food should be nourishing, enjoyable, and fun!

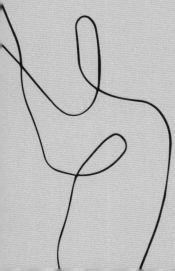

ABOUT THE AUTHOR

Since the age of four, I have been navigating life with severe food allergies like many others in the United States and our world at large. As a child, attending birthday parties, playdates, sporting events, and the like presented unique challenges and concerns to which many of my peers could not relate. The green lunchbox that housed my EpiPens and routine conversations with parents, teachers, and coaches helped me stay safe and feel like I could do just about anything, other than eat nuts of course. I took comfort in my environment when it was familiar and filled with family members, teachers, or trusted friends, but as I ventured into independence and new places on my own, my food allergy confidence often wavered.

Trying to eat in dining halls filled with nut-containing dishes and students who did not understand food allergies or cross-contact was difficult and a significant source of stress. Calling 911 as a freshman for a peer in anaphylaxis had a lasting impact on me and caused fear along with some paranoia to rule my life, which made going to class and socializing extremely difficult. While I have always been observant of my surroundings and know that I am probably more alert to the presence of nuts because of my allergies, at times it has felt like the world is out to get me. Going to college, I knew I would see nuts in dining halls and vending machines, but I did not expect to find myself dodging KIND bar crumbs in lecture halls, a jar of Nutella falling from a high-rise and exploding everywhere, or Snickers wrappers all over the laundry room. I did not anticipate receiving emails telling me to avoid the dining hall because it was "Peanut Day" or "Pistachio Day," and I was shocked when a cook hit me with a snarky "Oh yeah, I have dealt with you before," when I informed him of my allergy as instructed when ordering a chicken quesadilla. Maybe my expectations for the general public are a little too high for allergy awareness, cleanliness, and human decency. Maybe you agree with me and can relate to some of these frustrations or wish people were more considerate in general. Whichever the case may be, I choose to believe most people are good people. Many folks are willing to learn and even save their granola bar to eat between classes.

These anxiety-inducing experiences had me relying on my favorite seed-based granola and other nut-free snacks, microwaveable oatmeal, and food made by family members. Eating was no longer something I enjoyed and at times even safe food felt problematic. Crazy, I know. I learned how to stuff a mini fridge and had some microwave mishaps along the way while working to adjust an expensive meal plan that I was not using and obligated to have. Once I had an apartment and had access to a kitchen, I was excited to finally eat more "real" food again, but still on high alert as I shared this space with roommates. I kept things basic for peace of mind and convenience and reflected on how my nutrition at school differed from my norm at home. I began to wonder about the struggles of others with food allergies and felt thankful for the cooking knowledge I had, despite being nowhere near as competent as cooks like Ina Garten, Giada De Laurentiis, or even my dad, who never fails to provide a delicious meal.

NUT-FREE NUTRITION

In my experience, nutrition guidance for food allergies is often limited to avoiding allergens. More specifically, allergists encouraged my family members and I to read all ingredient lists and nutrition labels, make food from scratch, and to inform waitstaff of my allergies when eating out. In addition, I was told to avoid Asian foods, baked goods, pesto, marzipan, etc. Beyond this list, however, the only dietary recommendation I received was to "eat fruits and vegetables and make healthy choices!" As a college student studying nutrition, I began to wonder about my own needs and whether there were foods I should try to eat more of because I cannot eat nuts.

Nut are considered part of the "Protein Foods" group by the Dietary Guidelines for Americans, but they provide benefits beyond protein. Monounsaturated fats, such as oleic acid and polyunsaturated fats, such as linoleic and alpha-linolenic acid can be found in nuts, which makes them a heart healthy source of fat. Micronutrients, such as magnesium, potassium, copper, zinc, calcium, and phosphorus, along with vitamin E and several B vitamins (B3, B6, B9) are abundant. Certain compounds within nuts (e.g., flavonoids, tannins, phenolic acids, and isoflavones) may provide additional health benefits. Lastly, nuts are a good source of fiber, which is helpful for digestion and satiety.

After getting a better understanding of the nutrients in nuts, I set out on a quest to find foods that provide these nutrients, so I could better support my dietary needs. Many of the recipes in this book were inspired by my findings along with some other information I learned about the nutrition status of American adults and deficiencies college-aged adults may experience.

According to the Dietary Guidelines for Americans 2020-2025, all adults do not consume enough fruits and vegetables, or dairy products. American adults consume sufficient protein, but little comes from nuts, soy, and seeds as less than 50% consume the recommended amounts of these foods. Only about 10% of adults eat the recommended amount of seafood, and dietary fiber intakes are not fulfilled by over 90% of adults. Insufficient consumption of beans, peas and lentils likely contributes to the lack of fiber. These guidelines also reveal that 70-75% of Americans consume too much saturated fat.

While nutrient deficiencies can appear at any stage, young adults may experience deficiencies in vitamins E and D as well as calcium and iron. Meeting with a registered dietitian and speaking with a physician can help one identify and resolve any deficiencies and optimize their nutrition.

Foods containing the nutrients found in nuts are listed on the next page and may be valuable when making your meals. It must be acknowledged that those with nut allergies may be allergic to other foods (e.g., other legumes, seeds etc.). Discuss any concerns with your allergist, and do not hesitate to let others know all the foods you avoid.

FOODS TO INCLUDE

Seeds
Rich in minerals and high in polyunsaturated fats, seeds are nutrient dense and similar to nuts. Some of the many minerals provided by seeds are magnesium, zinc, iron, copper, and calcium.

Legumes
Beans, peas, and lentils are some of the many foods in the legume family. This group of food contains linoleic and alpha-linolenic acid, which are two essential fatty acids. Legumes also contain fiber, zinc, calcium, and iron. However, it is important to note that the bioavailability of iron is low, so other sources are necessary.

Fish and Shellfish
Seafood is high in protein and the essential fatty acids EPA and DHA. Individuals who are pregnant, planning to get pregnant, or breastfeeding should select options low in methylmercury. Salmon, anchovies, sardines, Pacific oysters, trout, tilapia, shrimp, catfish, crab, and flounder are some of the recommended options for low methylmercury.

Berries
Numerous minerals and vitamins can also be found in berries, and they also offer important fiber and contain polyphenols such as flavonoids, which may be beneficial for health.

Dried Fruits
Antioxidants such as flavonoids and tannins can be found in dried fruits along with vitamins E and B6. Folate (B9) and fiber can also be obtained from these foods, which include apricots, raisins, dates, and more.

References
Alasalvar, C., Salas-Salvadó, J., Ros, E., & Sabaté, J. (2020). Health Benefits of Nuts and Dried Fruits. Taylor & Francis Group.

Alasalvar, C., Salas-Salvadó, J., & Ros, E. (2020). Bioactives and health benefits of nuts and dried fruits. Food Chemistry, 314, 126192. https://doi.org/10.1016/j.foodchem.2020.126192
Dietary Guidelines for Americans, 2020-2025. (n.d.). 164.

Dodevska, M., Kukic Markovic, J., Sofrenic, I., Tesevic, V., Jankovic, M., Djordjevic, B., & Ivanovic, N. D. (2022). Similarities and differences in the nutritional composition of nuts and seeds in Serbia. Frontiers in Nutrition, 9, 1003125. https://doi.org/10.3389/fnut.2022.1003125

Dreher, M. L., Maher, C. V., & Kearney, P. (1996). The Traditional and Emerging Role of Nuts in Healthful Diets. Nutrition Reviews, 54(8), 241–245. https://doi.org/10.1111/j.1753-4887.1996.tb03941.x

Messina, M. J. (1999). Legumes and soybeans: Overview of their nutritional profiles and health effects. The American Journal of Clinical Nutrition, 70(3), 439s–450s. https://doi.org/10.1093/ajcn/70.3.439s

Ros, E., Tapsell, L. C., & Sabaté, J. (2010). Nuts and Berries for Heart Health. Current Atherosclerosis Reports, 12(6), 397–406. https://doi.org/10.1007/s11883-010-0132-5

Rose, A. M., Williams, R. A., Rengers, B., Kennel, J. A., & Gunther, C. (2018). Determining attitudinal and behavioral factors concerning milk and dairy intake and their association with calcium intake in college students. Nutrition Research and Practice, 12(2), 143–148. https://doi.org/10.4162/nrp.2018.12.2.143

Tangpricha, V., Pearce, E. N., Chen, T. C., & Holick, M. F. (2002). Vitamin D insufficiency among free-living healthy young adults. The American Journal of Medicine, 112(8), 659–662. https://doi.org/10.1016/S0002-9343(02)01091-4

Thomson, C. D., Chisholm, A., McLachlan, S. K., & Campbell, J. M. (2008). Brazil nuts: An effective way to improve selenium status. The American Journal of Clinical Nutrition, 87(2), 379–384. https://doi.org/10.1093/ajcn/87.2.379

Wan, Z., Wang, L., Xu, Y., Wang, Y., Zhang, T., Mao, X., Li, Q., Zhu, Y., Zhou, M., & Li, Z. (2021). Hidden Hunger of Vitamin E among Healthy College Students: A Cross- Sectional Study. Endocrine, Metabolic & Immune Disorders - Drug Targets(Formerly Current Drug Targets - Immune, Endocrine & Metabolic Disorders), 21(6), 1025–1030. https://doi.org/10.2174/1871530321666210101165648

bring on the
BREAKFAST

BREAKFAST

CHIA SEED PUDDING	10
SPINACH & PEPPER EGG BITES	11
HIGH PROTEIN FRENCH TOAST	13
SMOOTHIES	14
EPIC EGG SANDWICH	16
CHIA JAM BREAKFAST PASTRIES	18
OMELETS	21
SUPER SEEDY GRANOLA	23
WAFFLES	25
CINNAMON RAISIN OVERNIGHT OATS	28

Whether you're a busy student, a young adult taking on the professional world, or an individual enjoying some rest and relaxation, starting your day off with a good breakfast is important. Beginning your day with a meal gives your brain and muscles valuable energy and nutrients that help you accomplish tasks and stay focused. While supporting one's ability to learn new things, crush a workout, and power through exams, eating breakfast can help prevent mood swings and maintain normal body functions. Eating regular meals throughout the day and honoring hunger cues may also prevent overeating or poor food choices later in the day. Having protein, carbohydrates, and healthy fats at each meal is ideal for maintaining energy levels and satiety. Worth noting, some of these recipes are more well balanced while others should be served with another side for maximum nutrition.

In this section you will find a variety of recipes that aim to support your nutrition, satisfy your cravings, and help you to enjoy the many foods we nut-allergic individuals often cannot have. Some of these recipes are great for on the go, while others might be better for a weekend or day where you have more time to cook. When you have food allergies, it can be easy to get stuck eating the same things again and again, and while routine provides a sense of comfort and may reduce your anxiety, it can take some of the joy out of eating and make feelings of wanting to be "normal" more common. With that in mind, I encourage you to try some of these recipes so your list of go-tos gets a little longer, you do not feel that you are missing out on tasty foods, and your nutrition is a little bit better.

CHIA SEED PUDDING

TOTAL TIME: 2 HOURS | MAKES ½ CUP | SERVINGS: 1

Chia seeds are very nutritious as they contain fiber, unsaturated fats, and protein! These seeds contain essential fatty acids, omega-3 and omega-6, which must be obtained through diet, as the body cannot synthesize them. The high fiber content of chia seeds is what causes them to absorb so much liquid and develop a gelatinous texture. Fun fact: they can absorb 12 times their weight in liquid when soaked! With this recipe, you can stop wondering about the chia pudding you saw at that cute cafe with almond milk and peanut butter and add variety to your breakfast repertoire. Be sure to stay hydrated, though, as chia seeds will continue absorbing water in your stomach!

INGREDIENTS

½ cup milk*
2 tbsp chia seeds
pinch of salt
¼ tsp vanilla extract
1 tsp of maple syrup or honey
Berries, sliced banana for topping

DIRECTIONS

Take out a small glass, bowl, or storage container if you will be taking this on the go.

Add in the milk and other ingredients and stir until well combined.

Cover and place in the fridge overnight, or for a minimum of 2 hours.

Top with fresh berries, sliced banana, or other fruit as desired for extra nutrients and flavor.

STORAGE

Chia pudding will keep in the fridge for 4-5 days.

NOTES

*I use skim or reduced-fat milk, but you can also use fortified soy, hemp, or flax milk as they have more nutrients and are higher in protein than other nondairy options. If you can safely have coconut milk or prefer using oat milk, you might consider adding some yogurt to the mixture or having a protein on the side such as eggs or turkey bacon.

I suggest making multiple servings while you have the ingredients out, so you have breakfast made for a few days or a healthy snack easily available after class, practice, or a late-night study session.

SPINACH & PEPPER EGG BITES

TOTAL TIME: 30 MINUTES | MAKES 12 BITES | SERVINGS: 6

As a young adult, running out the door to class or work in a hurry might be part of your routine. While it is easy to just grab a bar or your favorite box of cereal and head out the door, waking up a little earlier or preparing food the night before can help you get in a quality breakfast and still get out the door on time. Egg bites are helpful to make ahead of time, so in the morning, all you will need to do is reheat them or pack them in a lunchbox to reheat once you have arrived at your destination.

INGREDIENTS

cooking spray*
12 large eggs
2 cups spinach
½ of a red bell pepper
½ tsp garlic powder
½ tsp salt
¼ tsp black pepper

Optional
2 tbsp skim milk
¾ cup reduced-fat feta cheese**

STORAGE

Store bites in an airtight container in the refrigerator for 3-5 days or freezer for up to 2 months.

NOTES

DIRECTIONS

Preheat your oven to 400°F and prepare your muffin tin with baking spray.

Rinse the pepper and spinach and chop. I recommend dicing the bell pepper and giving the spinach a rough chop so there aren't any huge leaves.

Crack the eggs into a medium-sized bowl and beat using a whisk or fork.

Add the seasonings to the eggs. For a creamier texture, extra protein, or a more mild egg taste, mix in 2 tbsp of milk.

Stir in the vegetables and combine.

Fill each muffin cup about ¾ of the way with the mixture and top with feta cheese if desired.

Bake for 15-20 minutes or until eggs are firm. Allow bites to cool for at least 5 minutes before removing from the pan.

*I normally use an olive or avocado spray but any kind will do.

**Reduced-fat cheese does not melt as well, so I suggest making small crumbles.

Reheat egg bites in the microwave for 30 seconds at a time or a few minutes in a toaster/air fryer when fresh. Reheat for about 5 minutes if frozen.

These egg bites are a great way to use up vegetables. I like using spinach and pepper because you don't need to cook them ahead of time. Broccoli, mushrooms, and onion would also work well, but I would cook them a little bit beforehand until tender.

A higher protein version of this recipe can be made using 2 cups of liquid egg whites and about ⅓ cup of cottage cheese. Cooking time may be a few minutes longer.

HIGH PROTEIN FRENCH TOAST

TOTAL TIME: 15 MINUTES | MAKES 4 PIECES | SERVINGS: 2

Waking up to the smell of French toast cooking was always a nice treat as a kid. Sometimes I could convince my mom to make some before school, but it was usually a weekend breakfast. Watching my mom make French toast was how I first learned to make it, but I got some extra practice in a high school cooking class. My bread of choice was always cinnamon raisin, which turned heads frequently. As I have grown older, I have learned to appreciate other breads too, but I think cinnamon raisin is still my favorite.

INGREDIENTS

4 slices of wheat bread*
2 large eggs
¼ cup egg whites, ~2 large eggs' worth
2 tbsp milk**
1 tsp vanilla extract
½ tsp cinnamon
olive or other cooking spray
maple syrup

DIRECTIONS

Crack your eggs into a shallow dish and beat with a fork or whisk.

Mix in the egg whites, milk, vanilla, and cinnamon. The cinnamon tends to stay at the surface, so add more if you need to as you go.

Soak slices of bread (both sides) in the dish for a minute or two while you prepare your pan with cooking spray and start heating it to medium.

Place slices of bread in the pan and cook them on medium heat for about 3-4 minutes per side or until your desired doneness. I recommend spraying the top side of the slices with a little cooking spray, so they do not stick when you flip them.

Serve hot with maple syrup.

STORAGE

Store leftovers in the fridge in a bag or airtight container for 3 days.

NOTES

*I like to use sprouted wheat bread with seeds as it has more protein and nutrients than white or whole wheat, but use your favorite. Breads often come with "may contain" or "made in a facility" statements, so keep an eye out for those.

**I use skim or reduced-fat milk, but fortified soy, hemp, or flax milk are good alternatives as they have some protein and nutrients that nondairy options often lack.

SMOOTHIES

TOTAL TIME: 10 MINUTES | SERVINGS: 1 12-OZ SMOOTHIE

Whether I am on a trip with my family, roaming around with friends, exploring aisles of the grocery store, or leaving the gym, smoothies seem to follow me everywhere. Their convenience and ability to provide important nutrition is something I admire, but most of the time I am filled with envy when smoothies are around as pretty much all smoothie sites have items that contain some sort of nut milk or nut butter. Let's not forget the granola and chopped nuts that make up the aesthetic smoothie bowl toppings! The presence of coconut milk and flakes might also be of concern for those with tree nut allergies who are also allergic to this drupe or advised against eating it.

Some places have separate blenders or wash their equipment thoroughly if a customer has an allergy, but who wants to risk it when they see the peanut butter protein powder on the top shelf, or hear the middle schoolers in front of them order a Reese's peanut butter cup shake and green smoothie with vanilla almond milk? Certainly not me.

Over the years, I have occasionally picked up a bottled fruit smoothie that was safe so I could try and get my smoothie fix and understand the hype. However, these store-bought smoothies were often underwhelming and loaded with sugar. I found many of them to be super runny, which was not satisfying as I tend to prefer a thicker texture for both taste and fullness purposes.

If you're an experienced smoothie fanatic, or you want to make one that is safe for you to bring to an early class or enjoy after a workout, I encourage you to check out the tips below, and these 3 recipes! Happy blending :)

SMOOTHIE TIPS

- Use a frozen banana for a thicker, creamier texture. Slicing before you freeze will make for easier blending!
- Frozen fruit helps thicken the smoothie and makes it cold without diluting it. If you only have fresh, add a few ice cubes to the blender.
- Yogurt, tofu, or protein powder can be added to increase protein, especially if you are not using dairy milk, or a fortified alternative (e.g., soy, flax milk).
- Protein powders are considered supplements, which means they are not regulated the same way food is. Their ability to cause digestive upset, especially in those who are lactose intolerant is another reason to be cautious when using them.
- Consider freezing bags of portioned ingredients to save some time.
- Shaking the blender pitcher can help the chunks of fruit get closer to the blade.
- Make sure to use enough liquid and add extra if needed for easy blending.
- Smoothies are best enjoyed fresh….time in the fridge can affect the color, taste, and texture, which can make them less appetizing and lead to food waste.

THE GREEN MACHINE

1 frozen banana
1 cup low-fat milk, fruit juice, or water
1 cup or generous handful of fresh spinach
½ cup frozen pineapple chunks
1 tbsp of flax seeds or flaxseed meal
Cacao nibs, berries for topping

CHOCOLATE BANANA BEAST

1 frozen banana
½ cup low-fat milk or alternative
2 tbsp sunflower seed butter
½ tsp vanilla extract
1 tbsp cocoa powder
Cocoa powder, dark chocolate chips, banana slices for topping

BERRIES & CREAM

1 frozen banana
¼ cup water
1 cup mixed berries or your favorite
⅔ cup nonfat Greek yogurt, ~1 small container
1 tbsp chia seeds
Fresh berries or additional seeds for topping

EPIC EGG SANDWICH

TOTAL TIME: 15 MINUTES | SERVINGS: 1

Having never experienced the convenience of grabbing an egg sandwich from typical chain restaurants when traveling or running late to class or work, I was excited to try my first breakfast sandwich. Despite being more time consuming to make my own, I often tell myself it is fortunate for my nutrition, and maybe even my tastebuds.

Finding safe breads can be challenging sometimes and thus a roadblock to many egg sandwiches! Whether it was finding a new variety of English muffin after my childhood-trusted brand changed their manufacturing, discovering that most healthier and seeded breads have warning labels for nuts, or being nauseated by the smell of fresh peanut butter and sight of numerous other nut spreads, the bread aisle can be tricky territory. With some research and careful reading, I have been able to find some safe options and enjoy sandwiches, French toast, and the like as a result. Special thanks to my dad and uncle who have made me safe egg sandwiches over the years!

The breakfast sandwich is similar to many foods in that everyone has their preferred method or ingredient combinations. Some people like bacon, others like sausage; some individuals only like a certain type of cheese, while others need a blend; We cannot forget about the "sauce people" and those who have a special order for stacking ingredients. Then, there are those who need to cut the sandwich a certain way or prefer eating it open-faced. Maybe you're like my cousin Bryan who likes making his egg sandwich with a toaster waffle instead of bread….it's actually really good! My point here is everyone's got unique taste, so have an open mind when it comes to ingredients and making your next egg sandwich.

INGREDIENTS

2 slices whole wheat bread, English muffin, or waffles*
1 egg, fried
¼ cup baby arugula
1-2 ¼" slices of tomato
1 oz reduced-fat cheddar cheese
cooking spray
black pepper

Optional
2 slices of tempeh
2 slices of pre cooked chicken or turkey bacon**

DIRECTIONS

Get out all of the ingredients that you plan to use so that it is easy to assemble the sandwich. Then, begin toasting your bread.

Once the bread is a little more than 50% toasted, spray your pan with cooking spray and turn it up to medium.

Then, crack your egg into the pan. Once most of the white is cooked, flip it over with a spatula and continue cooking until your desired level of doneness is achieved. I like to press down on it after I flip it so that the yolk is not runny.

At this point, lower the heat a little, and add the cheese to the top of the egg so that it can start melting a little bit. If you are using tempeh or precooked chicken or turkey bacon, add it to the pan now. You can also add the tomato slices if you prefer them cooked. Cook for 2-3 minutes.

When the cheese is melty, grab a plate and get your toast.

Place the egg on one half and sprinkle some black pepper on top. Don't worry if the cheese isn't entirely melted because the heat of the toast will help it keep melting.

Add the tomato, arugula, and tempeh or bacon if using, and close the sandwich with the other piece of toast.

Enjoy!

STORAGE

Best enjoyed fresh, but sandwiches can be stored in the fridge for four days or wrapped in foil for on the go eating. Just do not microwave foil as it is a fire hazard!!

NOTES

*Try the sandwich out with the waffle recipe found at the end of the chapter, or your favorite toaster waffles for a fun twist!

**Processed meats are often high in fat and sodium and increased consumption of these meats is associated with increased risk of colorectal cancer, which may be due to the presence of nitrates, nitrites, and other compounds. While chicken and turkey bacon are lower in fat, they still are not great for you. With this in mind, consider adding more produce instead like avocado or some roasted peppers, or try out a plant-based bacon alternative like tempeh!

If you do not have a toaster, or are concerned about cross contamination, use a larger pan that will fit the bread and the eggs or a second pan and start toasting it with some olive oil before cooking the egg. You can lean the bread against the side of the pan once toasted to keep it warm while you cook the egg!

CHIA JAM BREAKFAST PASTRIES

TOTAL TIME: 15 MINUTES | MAKES 8 PASTRIES | SERVINGS: 8

Enjoying a pastry from a café is something I very rarely get to experience due to the prevalence of nuts in baked goods at these locations. The sight of a case full of muffins and pastries has often had me wondering which I would like best if I could try them. These pastries are a healthier take on the packaged varieties many of us ate growing up. Although not as fancy as pastries one would find in a bakery, these are tastier and more nutritious than many choices on local grocery store shelves!

INGREDIENTS

2 cups whole wheat flour
½ tsp baking powder
½ tsp salt
1 tbsp granulated sugar
¼ cup milk*
⅓ cup olive or vegetable oil
1 large egg + 1 tbsp water
8 tbsp of chia jam**
powdered sugar for dusting

Optional glaze
¼ powdered sugar
3 tbsp Greek yogurt
2 tsp vanilla extract
1 tbsp water

DIRECTIONS

Preheat your oven to 400°F and line a baking sheet with parchment paper.

In a medium-sized bowl combine the flour, baking powder, salt, and sugar.

Stir in the milk and oil until a dough forms.

Once the liquid has been absorbed, separate the dough into 2 equal portions and wrap each section in wax paper or cover the bowl with plastic wrap.

Refrigerate the dough for 30 minutes and prepare the jam if needed (see next page).

Roll chilled dough on a floured surface and make a large 9x12-inch rectangle that's about ¼-inch thick. Use a knife to make edges straight.

Then, cut smaller rectangles that are about 3x4 inches and transfer them to your baking sheet.

Repeat with rhe other half of the dough. There should be 8 rectangles on each baking sheet.

CHIA JAM

TOTAL TIME: 10 MINUTES | MAKES ~1 CUP | SERVINGS: 16 (1-TBSP)

Making chia jam is a fun way to get more seeds into your diet! Sugar and pectin are often used to thicken jam, but with chia seeds, you don't need either! Add this lower sugar jam to oatmeal, sandwiches, cookies, yogurt bowls and more!

INGREDIENTS

2 cups of your favorite berry, fresh or frozen
2 tbsp chia seeds
1 tbsp fresh lemon juice
2 tbsp honey or agave if needed

DIRECTIONS

Add 2 cups of your favorite berries to a saucepan and cook on medium heat while stirring frequently as the berries cook down.

Using the back of a spoon, fork, or potato masher, mash the berries to your desired consistency. Keep in mind that the chia seeds will absorb liquid and help to thicken the jam.

Once the berries have reached your desired consistency, remove the pan from the heat and add in the lemon juice.

If the berries are too tart, add in some honey or agave (about 2 tbsp).

Shut off the heat and let the jam cool for a few minutes before filling pastries or adding to a container for later use.

STORAGE

Store chia jam in an airtight container in the refrigerator for 5-7 days.

NOTES

Chia seeds can absorb 10-12 times their weight in water, which means they will absorb water from the fruit and your stomach. Staying on top of your water intake can prevent indigestion.

Beat the egg and water together in a small bowl. Use a brush or clean fingers to brush each piece lightly with the egg wash. Save the remaining wash for later.

Add 1 tablespoon of chia jam to the middle of 8 rectangles, and use the back of a spoon to spread the jam out a bit. Place the other pastry rectangles on top of those with the jam.

Crimp the edges with a fork so the filling does not ooze out. Poke a few holes on top to let the steam escape.

Apply the remaining egg wash to the top of each pastry and bake for 15-20 minutes at 400°F or until the tops brown.

Remove from the oven and cool.

Combine the ingredients for the glaze and apply a thin layer, or dust with powdered sugar if desired.

STORAGE

Keep pastries in an airtight container at room temperature for 3 days or in the refrigerator for a week.

NOTES

*I use skim or reduced-fat milk, but fortified soy, hemp, or flax milk are good alternatives as they are nut-free and have some protein and nutrients that nondairy options often lack.

**If you do not have time to make the jam or want to try different flavors, you can use chopped apples with cinnamon, melted chocolate, or cinnamon sugar for the filling instead!

OMELETS

TOTAL TIME: 15 MINUTES | SERVINGS: 1

When it comes to dining out for breakfast, I tend to choose an omelet or egg-centric dish as this section of the menu tends to be clear of nuts. When I was little, my dad would make me omelets sometimes on the weekends, and when I would eat breakfast at the dining halls at school, the omelet station was my spot. Well, it was most students' spot actually, as the customizable, filling, and almost home-cooked nature of omelets was extremely appealing to tired, hungry students. I valued the omelet station because I knew the only foods there were veggies, eggs, meats, and cheese, and everyone approached with an empty plate so there was minimal concern for me. Because I frequented "Omelet Land," the workers became friendly faces I looked forward to seeing while away from home, and one of them always made sure to tell me when they had goat cheese as it was a rare occasion and she knew I loved it.

I would say my omelet skills are still developing, but I strive to one day be an omelet expert. The beauty about omelets is that you can switch up the filling when you get bored or need to use up specific ingredients in your kitchen. They can also be a nutritious option as they contain protein, some healthy fats, fiber, and micronutrients. Being mindful of the type and how much cheese can be helpful as cheese contains saturated fat and sodium. Processed meats like bacon and sausage also add additional saturated fat and sodium, despite being very tasty, so keep this in mind if you're an omelet lover.

INGREDIENTS

2 large eggs, or 3 egg whites
1 tbsp milk*
about ½ cup veggies**
2 oz reduced-fat cheese***
olive oil or cooking spray

DIRECTIONS

Cut up your veggies into small pieces. If using spinach, you may want to chop up the leaves; although, they will still cook down if you skip this step.

Add a tiny bit of olive oil or spray to your pan and cook your veggies on low medium heat until they start to get tender. About 3-5 minutes.

While the veggies cook, crack the eggs into a small bowl and beat with a fork or whisk. Add in a splash of milk if you like. If you are dairy-free, you can substitute water to help your eggs fluff.

Once the veggies are ready, spread them out in the pan and add a little more cooking spray if needed. Pour the egg mixture overtop and turn up the heat a tiny bit.

Some of my favorites:

¼ cup cherry tomatoes, chopped
½ cup spinach (cooks down a lot)
goat cheese

¼ cup broccoli florets, chopped
2 tbsp white or yellow onion, diced
¼ cup mushrooms, sliced
cheddar cheese

3 asparagus spears, chopped
1 tbsp scallion, diced
provolone cheese

2 tbsp red bell pepper, diced
2 tbsp white or yellow onion, diced
1 tbsp crispy chicken bacon pieces
cheddar cheese

Let the eggs cook, and after a few minutes, lift up the edges of the egg so that liquid from the top will flow over and cook. It may help to carefully tilt the pan a bit.

When the eggs look mostly cooked, flip the eggs over with a spatula.

Place your cheese of choice on half of the eggs and with your spatula fold the other half on top.

You can continue flipping until your desired doneness is achieved.

Serve right away.

Omelets are a great way to get in a lot of nutrients and you can fill yours with whatever you like! I'm confident that most veggies will work if you are in a pinch. Although, carrots and celery probably would not be the most flavorful option. To all my avocado fans, I suggest keeping it on the side, rather than in the omelet as hot avocado chunks are kind of gross (Thank you, Logan Airport for that lesson).

STORAGE

Omelets are best when made fresh. They can be stored in the fridge for 3 days, but I suggest making them the day of to avoid soggy eggs. Reheat them on the stove.

NOTES

*Fortified soy, hemp, or flax milk are good nondairy, nut-free options for this recipe.

**Use any vegetables you like or have on hand and add more or less depending on your preference.

***Reduced-fat cheese doesn't always melt easily, so you may want to shred it finely. If you are lactose intolerant or dairy free use a substitution that is safe for you, or just skip the cheese all together!

Prior to attending college, I would add cooked veggies to the eggs while they cooked before adding the cheese. I now prefer the veggies cooked into the egg as it keeps the filling from falling out when you cut it. Try it both ways to see what you like best!

SUPER SEEDY GRANOLA

TOTAL TIME: 60 MINUTES | MAKES 12 SERVINGS (⅓ CUP)

It was not until I found a safe seed-based granola that I actually understood the hype around this food. Granola just seemed like bird food that humans ate when they wanted to be healthy. What could possibly be so good about something so crunchy it might break your teeth? The fact that my parents never mentioned missing it in our nut-free home and my youthful passion for Lucky Charms and other cereals kept me from exploring a homemade version. Nut-free granolas at the store are hard to come by and have ingredients limited to oats, honey, chocolate chips, and sometimes fruit. While I am extremely grateful for the brands making certified allergen-free granolas, they are not always accessible and can be expensive. Those without seeds were really just providing flavorful carbs and texture to my yogurt bowls, without many other nutrients, so with convenience, nutrition, and my bank account in mind, I set out to make nut-free granola. After several attempts, I think I finally got it right. Consider this recipe your invitation to the granola hype train and inspiration for your own granola ventures.

INGREDIENTS

2 cups rolled oats
½ cup unsalted pumpkin seeds
2 tbsp flax seeds
2 tbsp chia seeds
2 tbsp hemp seeds
⅓ cup maple syrup or honey
⅓ cup olive oil
1 tsp cinnamon
½ tsp vanilla extract
¼ tsp salt

DIRECTIONS

Line a baking sheet with parchment paper and preheat oven to 350°F.

Combine oats and seeds in a large bowl.

Heat sweetener of choice and oil in a pan over medium heat for 2-4 minutes, or until you see some bubbles. Don't let it burn.

Pour mixture over the oats and seeds and stir until everything is coated. Mix in cinnamon, vanilla, and salt.

Spread into a rectangle on your baking sheet and press it down with a spatula.

Bake 20-25 minutes at 350°F or until golden and mostly dry.

Remove from oven, press with spatula, and let it dry for 30-40 minutes.

Break into pieces and add to your favorite yogurt, enjoy it with milk, or by the handful!

STORAGE

Keep granola in an airtight container for about a week! I recommend using a mason jar or a container that you can pour out of instead of a plastic bag, but anything that seals will do!

NOTES

The following information can be very helpful when making granola with clusters!

Minimal to no stirring at the halfway point. I know we want the pieces toasted evenly, but this can reduce the cluster potential. If you do stir, definitely press down with your spatula again to help ingredients stick.

Let it dry for a good while before you break it into pieces.

Heating the liquid into a "sauce" can help it stick together.

Adding egg whites can help ingredients stick and increases the protein content.

It comes out better if you cook it at a lower temperature for longer, so do not try and rush the process.

Stir in chocolate chips and any dried fruit after breaking it into clusters so the chocolate does not melt.

Use gluten-free oats if you or someone you love has celiac disease, a wheat allergy, or gluten intolerance.

Substitute avocado or vegetable oil if you do not have olive oil. Coconut oil can also work if it is safe for you, but know that it is high in saturated fats, which increase LDL cholesterol and are harmful for heart health.

WAFFLES

TOTAL TIME: 30 MINUTES | MAKES 8-7" waffles | SERVINGS: 4

One of my favorite questions to ask people is: how would you rank French toast, pancakes, and waffles? For me, the best French toast ever would probably take first place, but I find it's often hard for restaurants to do really well, and if you get those eggy pieces...forget about it. I do enjoy pancakes, but I am not as thrilled by them now due to my family's tradition of eating them every Sunday (Sorry, Mom & Dad). My appreciation for waffles is probably more than most people's — my own surveys reveal they're usually #2 or #3. It's okay, I'm proud of it. I'm sure part of it's the nostalgic memories eating toaster waffles with vanilla ice cream and blueberry sauce for dessert, or the greatness that is butter and syrup being held by the pockets. Something about waffles just reminds me of home and puts a smile on my face, and I hope this recipe brings one to yours. And just to clarify, it's 1. Waffles, 2. French toast, and 3. Pancakes.

INGREDIENTS

2 ¼ cups all purpose flour
½ tsp salt
1 tbsp baking powder
1 tsp cinnamon
3 tbsp sugar
2 tbsp flaxseed meal
2 large eggs
½ cup olive or vegetable oil
2 cups of milk*
2 tsp vanilla extract

Topping Recommendations
fresh berries, banana slices
chocolate chips
syrup or honey
butter or plant-based spread
seed butter

DIRECTIONS

Begin by combining the flour, salt, baking powder, cinnamon, sugar, and flaxseed meal in a medium-sized bowl.

Before proceeding to the next step, plug in your waffle iron so it can start preheating.

Next separate the eggs and beat the whites using an electric mixer or whisk until they turn white and form peaks. This should take about 2-3 minutes if using a mixer. Set egg whites aside, and add the 2 yolks to a large mixing bowl.

Add the oil to the egg yolks and whisk together along with the remaining wet ingredients: milk and vanilla extract.

Slowly add the dry ingredients into the wet ingredients and continue whisking.

Once the wet and dry mixtures are combined, take a spatula and fold in the egg whites until incorporated throughout. Do not overmix.

Add the batter to the heated waffle iron and cook according to the instructions for your appliance. If your waffle iron requires non-stick spray, be sure to use it. For reference, I use about ⅓ cup of batter for my iron.

Throw on any toppings or add a side of fruit if desired. Enjoy right away!

GLUTEN & DAIRY FREE WAFFLES

TOTAL TIME: 30 MINUTES | MAKES 8-7" waffles | SERVINGS: 4

Having a family member with celiac disease and a friend with a dairy allergy, I also wanted to share a waffle recipe I created for one of my nutrition classes that is free of gluten and dairy. The more waffles the better, right? Give it a try if you follow a gluten and/or dairy free diet, or if you just want to switch things up.

INGREDIENTS

2 cup gluten-free oat flour**
½ tsp salt
1 tbsp baking powder
1 tsp cinnamon
2 large eggs
1 cup nondairy milk***
¼ cup olive or vegetable oil
3 tbsp maple syrup
1 tsp vanilla extract

DIRECTIONS

Mix all dry ingredients in a medium-sized bowl.

Before proceeding to the next step, plug in your waffle iron so it can start preheating.

Separate the eggs, and beat the whites using an electric mixer or whisk until they form white peaks. This should take about 2-3 minutes if using a mixer. Set egg whites aside, and add the 2 yolks to a large mixing bowl.

Beat the egg yolks with a fork or whisk. Then, add the oat milk, oil, maple syrup and vanilla. Mix well.

Slowly add the dry ingredients into the wet ingredients and continue whisking. Finally, fold in the egg whites with a spatula.

Add the batter to the heated waffle iron and cook according to the instructions for your appliance. If your waffle iron requires non-stick spray, be sure to use it. For reference, I use about ⅓ cup of batter for my iron.

Add toppings as desired and enjoy!

STORAGE

If you plan to eat leftover waffles soon, keep them in an airtight container or storage bag, or wrapped in tinfoil in the fridge for 3 days. Waffles can also be kept in the freezer for up to 3 months. I suggest putting parchment paper between waffles or wrapping them individually. Cool waffles for 30 minutes before storing them to prevent sogginess.

NOTES

*I use skim or reduced-fat milk, but fortified soy, hemp, or flax milk are good alternatives as they have some protein and nutrients that nondairy options often lack. Oat milk will also work, but is lower in protein and often unfortified. I recommend the second recipe if you want dairy-free waffles.

**For these waffles to be glutenfree, certified gluten-free oats must be used. You can blend oats if you do not have store-bought oat flour. Another gluten-free flour can also be substituted for either recipe.

***I think oat milk works best in this recipe, but you can use another nondairy option (see above).

Vegetable oil may be preferred as it has a more neutral flavor, but olive oil does not affect the taste or texture much.

If you do not have an electric mixer, you can beat egg whites with a whisk; although, it will take longer and tire your arms! Beating the egg whites makes them light and airy, which leads to lighter waffles. I highly recommend doing this, but it can be skipped.

A "flax egg" substitute can be used if you are out of eggs or allergic. Just add the flaxeed meal to a small bowl with 5 tablespoons of water, mix, and let it sit for 7-10 minutes until it thickens (1 egg = 1 tbsp ground flax seeds: 2½ tbsp room temperature water). You can apply this same concept to the second recipe for a vegan waffle recipe!

To keep waffles hot, place them in the oven at 150°F spread out on a baking sheet. This can be helpful when serving multiple people so that everyone can eat together!

Frozen waffles can be reheated using a toaster, microwave, or oven.

CINNAMON RAISIN OVERNIGHT OATS

TOTAL TIME: 2 HOURS | MAKES 1 CUP | SERVINGS: 1

As a kid, I loved cereal. Well to be honest, I still love cereal...I wrote a college essay about different kinds if that's any indication of my love for this food. To my surprise, I eventually became an oatmeal person. In conversation, I quickly learned that many people dislike hot oatmeal due to the texture and taste. Overnight oats are a filling breakfast alternative to a classic bowl of sugary cereal and make a nice option for anyone who is averse to hot oatmeal. The great thing about this recipe is that it's easily customizable, so if you are not a raisin person, you can add your preferred mix-ins.

INGREDIENTS

½ cup rolled oats
½ cup milk*
½ tsp cinnamon
½ tsp vanilla extract
1-2 tsp maple syrup or honey
1 tbsp of raisins

Optional toppings/mix-ins
fresh berries
banana slices
seed butter
seeds
cacao nibs
protein powder**
Greek yogurt

DIRECTIONS

The night before you intend to have this breakfast, take out a bowl, glass, or mason jar. I recommend a container with a lid for easy packing in a lunch bag or on the go eating.

Add the oats, your milk of choice, cinnamon, vanilla extract, sweetener, and raisins to the container and mix it all together until everything is mixed.

Cover with a lid, or plastic wrap and place in the fridge overnight. If making this at a different time, I recommend leaving it in the fridge for a couple of hours, but overnight is best.

In the morning, add toppings if you like and enjoy!

STORAGE

Keep in the fridge in an airtight container for 4-5 days.

NOTES

*I use skim or reduced-fat milk, but you can also use fortified soy, hemp, or flax milk as they have more nutrients and are higher in protein than other nondairy options. If you can safely have coconut milk or prefer using oat milk, you might consider adding some yogurt or seeds to the mixture as these options have less protein.

**You can add protein powder, but it can be difficult to digest, especially if you are lactose intolerant. Protein powders are also not regulated the same way food is because they are considered supplements, so proceed with caution.

I suggest making multiple servings while you have the ingredients out, so you have breakfast made for a few days or a healthy snack easily available after class, practice, or a late-night study session.

If you do not like raisins, or prefer a lower sugar option, throw some fresh berries in instead.

Increasing the milk up to 1 cup will increase the protein and moisture content, so play around with the ratios and see which version you prefer.

let's do LUNCH

LUNCH

SIMPLE TUNA SALAD	33
SUNFLOWER BUTTER & JAM SANDWICH	34
CHICKEN CAESAR SALAD WRAPS	35
BLACK BEAN VEGGIE BURGERS	37
TASTY TOASTS	39
MEDITERRANEAN MEATBALLS & CHICKPEA SALAD	40
AWESOME ANTIOXIDANT SANDWICH	42
MINESTRONE SOUP	44
SHRIMP & SALSA LETTUCE WRAPS	46
CAULIFLOWER FLATBREADS	48

Whether you are out and about or rushing from one thing to the next, finding a safe option for lunch can be difficult. Hitting the dining hall might be challenging due to a lack of sufficient labeling, concerns about cross-contact, or even the anxiety of eating alone. A chain restaurant or fast-food location that understands allergies may not be easily accessible or somewhere you want to eat day after day for both nutritional and allergy concerns. Eating at friends' and family members' houses can be safe if they understand your needs, but many people lack sufficient knowledge about food allergies, and the prevalence of nut butters, trail mixes, nut-based milks, and granola in our peers' homes can make trusting food prepared away from our "bubble" really hard. That said, always listen to your gut.

Many of us nut-allergic individuals grew up eating lunches at the nut-free table and bringing bagged lunches on field trips. Turning down foods offered by peers at school and work and speaking to food service workers about our life-threatening allergies are actions that are just normal to us. Lunch may be the most inconvenient meal of the day for us because we can't easily run to a cafe or restaurant without the fear of having a reaction that may put our lives at risk or a wave of anxiety with the capacity to interrupt our productivity.

While everyone has different levels of comfort when it comes to eating in cafeterias, dining halls, restaurants, and shared kitchens, I believe that the best option is to pack your own lunch for school and the office or anywhere safe food might not be easily accessible. Sure, preparing lunches can be tiring and maybe inconvenient if you are super busy or not someone who enjoys being in the kitchen. However, food prepared at home is often more nutritious as takeout can be loaded with extra sodium, sugar, and unhealthy fats. So, while it may be easy to fixate on the ease with which your peers can grab a quick bite, I encourage you to remind yourself that you can eat nutritious and tasty food...and you might be a better cook too ;)

Having snacks and food packed for trips and social excursions can sometimes be helpful for reducing the stress around food. Worrying about access to safe food can be pretty consuming, especially when friends and family may make comments like, "I just don't know what to feed you!" or are unable to offer allergy-friendly food. If you feel comfortable cooking with someone else in their kitchen or at your place, ask if you can pick the recipe or recommend one. It's also important to discuss the safety of the environment beforehand and your allergy medications so there are no surprises and everyone is on the same page to keep you safe.

These nut-free lunches will keep you going throughout the day and can make for great on the go options so that you can eat between class, with your colleagues, at a friend or family member's house, and anywhere else on the road! Of course, you can make and enjoy any of these recipes without traveling anywhere, but I encourage you to go see what's out there and enjoy experiencing life. Pack a cooler, a lunchbox, a backpack, whatever you want, and go have a picnic at the beach, attend that sporting event on the weekend, meet up with some friends, or go play cards with your grandparents while enjoying good conversation. If it's better to eat before, at home, do that. Be smart, be safe, and do what makes you comfortable, but do not let your allergies keep you from doing what you love and socializing with the people who matter to you.

SIMPLE TUNA SALAD

TOTAL TIME: 10 MINUTES | SERVINGS: 2

When you need to make lunch quickly, a tuna salad sandwich can come in clutch. Tuna is high in protein, which will satisfy your appetite, and carbohydrates in the bread will give you energy to power through the rest of the day! I must admit that I was not always on Team Tuna. I mean, let's be honest, it's a little stinky. If you can get past the smell and muster the courage to try it, you might have a new lunch option!

INGREDIENTS

1 can your preferred tuna (look for low-sodium, no salt added)
2 tbsp light mayonnaise
1 tbsp white vinegar
1 celery stalk
salt and pepper if desired

STORAGE

Keep leftovers sealed in the fridge for 3-5 days.

DIRECTIONS

Open your tuna and strain the water and add to a small bowl. If your tuna is packed in olive or soybean oil you may also want to strain some of the liquid so that the salad has some body and isn't soupy, but do not worry if some remains as these oils contain heart healthy fats. If your tuna is packed without liquid just go ahead and add it straight to the bowl.

Next, add in your desired amount of mayonnaise. If using tuna that was packed in oil, it may not need as much so start off with a small amount and add until it is your desired texture.

Stir in 1 tablespoon of white vinegar.

Add 1 stalk of chopped celery for some crunch and fiber.

Sprinkle in some salt and pepper for extra flavor if desired.

Place about half the mixture, or your desired amount onto some whole wheat bread with toppings of your choice. If you prefer, you can spread it onto some crackers or rice cakes.

SUNFLOWER BUTTER & JAM SANDWICH

TOTAL TIME: 10 MINUTES | SERVINGS: 1

This sweet and savory duo is one I never thought I'd eat. I spent many years resisting sunflower butter as it reminded me too much of peanut butter. In 5th grade I had to kindly explain to a defensive classmate that he could not eat his almond butter sandwich at the nut-free table, and even now it still feels like everyone and their mother is addicted to nut butters. If seed or soy butter is safe for your allergies, this sandwich is a tasty place to start.

INGREDIENTS

2 slices whole wheat or multigrain bread
1-2 tbsp of sunflower seed butter
1-2 tbsp of your jam of choice* (see chia jam recipe on p. 19)

STORAGE

Eat right away or pack for lunch on the go! I suggest wrapping in tinfoil or using a container.

DIRECTIONS

Take your two pieces of bread and place them on a plate or clean cutting board. If you prefer to use toast, toast the bread before proceeding.

Spread your jam on one slice of bread to your desired thickness.

After cleaning the knife, repeat the previous step with the sunflower seed butter.

Put the slices together so the two spreads are touching.

Cut if desired and enjoy! If packing for a lunch on the go, consider toasting the bread and waiting to cut it to prevent sogginess and a sticky mess.

NOTES

*If you prefer, you can use jelly instead. The two spreads have virtually the same nutritional value, but jelly is often made from fruit juice, while jam is made from real fruit. I prefer the texture of jam, but use whichever you prefer, and consider making it from home for a lower sugar option!

I recommend having your own jam/jelly and labeling it if you are sharing a fridge with others or keeping it in your own mini fridge if you have one to avoid cross-contact. Roommates and friends might not think to use a separate knife, so this can be helpful.

CHICKEN CAESAR SALAD WRAPS

TOTAL TIME: 25 MINUTES | MAKES ABOUT 4 WRAPS | SERVINGS: 4

There's something about a chicken Caesar salad wrap that always brings a smile to my face. Maybe it's the crispy croutons, tasty dressing, or the nostalgia of eating these after basketball practice with friends growing up, I'm not really sure. While extremely tasty, this lunchtime favorite often gets a bad rap (yes, pun intended), as Caesar dressing is often high in sodium and fat, and the chicken might be breaded too, depending on where you get it from. When ordering out, it is common to find salads with nuts, and if you're like me, you might feel the need or desire to steer clear. With my longtime love of this dish and interest in safe food with a healthier spin, I wanted to share this recipe with you.

INGREDIENTS

For the Caesar dressing
2 cloves garlic
2 tsp anchovies
3 tbsp lemon juice, about 1 small lemon's worth
3 tbsp light mayonnaise
2 tsp Grey Poupon mustard
1 ½ tbsp olive oil
1 tbsp water
⅓ cup nonfat plain Greek yogurt
3 tbsp grated Romano cheese
¼ tsp pepper

For the chicken
2 tbsp olive or avocado oil
1 lb chicken breasts
salt and pepper to taste

DIRECTIONS

Mince the garlic, finely chop the anchovies, and juice your lemon and add them all to a small bowl or container.

Add the mayonnaise, mustard, oil, water, yogurt, cheese, and pepper. Stir well until the ingredients are combined and you have a smooth texture.

Cover with plastic wrap or a lid and place in the fridge while you cook the chicken.

Heat your oil in a skillet on medium heat.

Add your chicken breasts to the hot skillet and season with salt and pepper. If you like, you can add some dried basil for additional flavor, but with the dressing and croutons, it is not necessary.

Cook for 5-8 minutes a side, depending on thickness, on medium-high heat. Keep an eye on them and slice through the thickest part of the breast to check for doneness.

For homemade croutons (optional...but recommended)
2 cups cubed bread, any kind will do, but whole wheat or multigrain is more nutritious
2 tbsp olive oil
1 tsp dried basil
1 tsp garlic powder
½ tsp dried oregano

Other
4 whole wheat wraps*

Preheat the oven to 350°F and line a small baking sheet with parchment paper.

Cube your bread and place pieces in a small bowl.

Add the oil and seasonings and transfer to the baking sheet.

Bake for about 7 minutes or until golden brown. I recommend stirring them about halfway through.

Remove from the oven and set aside to cool.

I like to use 3-4 oz of chicken per wrap along with 1 cup of washed romaine torn into pieces, ¼ cup croutons, and 1-2 tablespoons of dressing. Stirring in a small bowl helps to make sure everything is well-coated. Place the mixture on your favorite wrap, or enjoy it as a salad if you prefer. I recommend trying whole wheat wraps if you can find some that are safe as they contain additional fiber and more protein.

STORAGE

I find it is best to store the ingredients separately so nothing becomes soggy. The dressing will last about 7 days, and the chicken should be consumed within 4 days... although, I doubt either will last that long!

NOTES

*You can use any wraps or pitas that are safe for you. Always remember to read the packaging because breads and the like can be tricky as ingredients and/or manufacturing practices can change!

BLACK BEAN VEGGIE BURGERS

TOTAL TIME: 40 MINUTES | MAKES 4-5 BURGERS | SERVINGS: 4-5

If you told me to eat a veggie burger several years ago, I likely would have resisted. Even as a veggie lover, I just didn't think a burger made from beans could satisfy me the same way one from beef could. The truth is, the more I tried different varieties and learned about the benefits of plant-based eating, the more I started to enjoy them. While there are many burger substitutes at the store that more closely mimic beef, I prefer to make mine so I can taste the individual ingredients. While I still like a real burger every so often, I'm definitely glad I am no longer a veggie burger snob and enjoy making these.

INGREDIENTS

1 15-oz can low-sodium or no salt added black beans
¼ cup, ~¼ of a larger bell pepper
½ cup, ~¼ of a large yellow onion
2 cloves garlic
1 tbsp olive or avocado oil
½ tsp chili powder
½ tsp paprika
¼ cup breadcrumbs
1 large egg
2 tbsp ketchup
2 tbsp Romano cheese
salt and pepper to taste

DIRECTIONS

Preheat the oven to 350°F and line a baking sheet with parchment paper. Strain and rinse black beans and spread evenly across the baking sheet. Bake for 10-15 minutes or until the beans are dried out.

Dice the bell pepper and onion and mince the garlic. Keep the onions and garlic separate as the peppers will take longer to cook.

While the beans are in the oven, add the olive oil to a pan and begin sautéing the veggies over medium heat. Start with the pepper, then add the onion and garlic after a few minutes. This will take about 5-6 minutes.

Transfer veggies to a large bowl. Mix in chili powder, paprika, breadcrumbs, egg, ketchup, and cheese. Add the beans when done cooking.

Turn the oven up to 375°F and get a new piece of parchment for the baking sheet if necessary.

Use a whisk or spoon to mash the beans and veggies a bit. A food processor or blender can be used for this too.

Form and place burger patties and on the baking tray. Use about ⅓ cup of mixture per burger and shape into desired thickness. Makes 4-5 patties.

Bake the burgers at 375°F for 20 minutes and flip them halfway through. They are done when the top and bottom have been browned.

Assemble a burger with your favorite toppings and enjoy!

STORAGE

Keep leftover burgers in a bag or airtight container in the fridge for 5 days. Burgers can be kept in the freezer for up to 3 months. I recommend cooking them first if you plan to freeze them.

NOTES

These are great to have on a salad or in a wrap too!

You can also cook these in a pan on medium-high heat for about 5 minutes a side, or until they are browned, instead of baking them.

TASTY TOASTS

TOTAL TIME: 10 MINUTES | SERVINGS: 1

When you are looking for a quick bite or easy lunch to throw together during the week, give tasty toasts a try! This is a fun way to take the typical trendy avocado toast to the next level or try out other nutritious toppings instead of putting butter or cream cheese on a bagel or a grilled cheese. I enjoy making these as I often cannot get fun sandwiches or avocado toast from restaurants because the bread is usually not safe. I also like this concept because it is a nutritious option that does not require a bunch of cooking, and it can involve as many ingredients as you want.

INGREDIENTS

Cucumber Salmon Toast
whole grain toast, pita, or English muffin
2 tbsp low-fat ricotta, or cottage cheese
2-3 oz smoked salmon, ~2 slices
capers
cucumber, sliced

Honey Avocado Toast
whole grain toast, pita, or English muffin
2 tbsp low-fat ricotta, or cottage cheese
avocado, sliced
green onion, sliced
honey
red pepper flakes

DIRECTIONS

Toast your bread.

Spread ricotta or cottage cheese onto the toast.

Place desired toppings on the toast and you're ready to eat!

STORAGE

I recommend eating these toasts right away or making them a few hours in advance and packing them in a lunchbox with an ice pack. If desired, store in the refrigerator for a maximum of 3 days, but know that the salmon and avocado will not be as fresh nor as tasty.

MEDITERRANEAN MEATBALLS & CHICKPEA SALAD

TOTAL TIME: 40 MINUTES | MAKES 24 MEATBALLS | SERVINGS: ~6

These chicken meatballs are light, refreshing, and super flavorful. If you want a lunch or dinner ready to go during the week, these are great! Chicken is a lean source of protein and contains less saturated fat than red meat, which makes these meatballs a healthier alternative to those made with beef. With some chickpea salad and starch of your choice, you will feel like you are at one of those trendy lunch spots, except you made the food!

INGREDIENTS

For the meatballs
1.5 lb ground chicken or turkey
1 cup red onion, diced
½ cup feta cheese crumbles
3 cloves garlic, minced
1 tbsp fresh mint, chopped
2 tsp dried oregano
½ cup fresh parsley, chopped
1 tbsp olive oil
salt and pepper to taste

For the chickpea salad*
1 15-oz can low-sodium chickpeas, rinsed and drained
1 avocado
1 ½ cups cherry tomatoes, halved
1 English cucumber, chopped
Juice of 1 lemon
3 tbsp olive oil
¼ cup fresh cilantro
1 clove of garlic, minced
½ tsp salt
¼ tsp ground black pepper

DIRECTIONS

Preheat your oven to 400°F and line a baking sheet with parchment paper.

Add the chicken to a large bowl and break apart with a spoon so it will be easier to add in the other ingredients.

Combine the red onion, cheese, garlic, mint, oregano, parsley, olive oil, and salt and pepper with the chicken. Using clean hands can make this process easier.

Roll the mixture into 2-inch balls and place on the prepared baking sheet. Using a scoop or tablespoon can be helpful for consistent sizes.

Once all of the meatballs have been placed on the baking sheet, place them in the oven for 25 minutes or until they begin to brown.

While the meatballs are baking, prepare the chickpea salad!

Combine the chickpeas, avocado, tomatoes, and cucumber in a medium bowl.

In another bowl, mix together the lemon juice, olive oil, cilantro, garlic, salt, and pepper.

Add the dressing to the salad until it meets your desired taste.

If you like sauces and dips, use the following recipe to make homemade Tzatziki!

TZATZIKI

TOTAL TIME: 5 MINUTES | MAKES ABOUT 2 CUPS | SERVINGS: ~8

INGREDIENTS

½ English cucumber shredded or diced
1 cup Greek yogurt
1 tbsp fresh dill chopped
1 cloves minced garlic
1 tbsp lemon juice
salt and pepper to taste

DIRECTIONS

Shred or dice your cucumber and place in a small bowl. Press the cucumber with a paper towel or cheesecloth to remove some moisture.

Add the yogurt, dill, garlic, lemon juice, salt and pepper to the cucumber and stir.

Serve the meatballs with rice, quinoa, or pita bread. Enjoy with the chickpea salad and tzatziki, olives, pickled cabbage, or any other toppings you love!

STORAGE

Store leftover meatballs in an airtight container or sealed bag for up to 5 days. The chickpea salad will be best within 1-2 days, but if you leave out the avocado, it may last a bit longer. Store your tzatziki in an airtight container for 5 days in the fridge.

NOTES

*The chickpea salad will yield around 6 cups, which is enough for 6 servings.

If you are unsure as to whether you like tzatziki, I recommend cutting the recipe in half, but otherwise this amount will last you a few meals, and it can be used as a dip with fresh vegetables, crackers, or pita too!

AWESOME ANTIOXIDANT SANDWICH

TOTAL TIME: 10-40 MINUTES | SERVINGS: 1

Not in the mood for a salad? Sick of your usual sandwich? Give the Awesome Antioxidant Sandwich a try to pack in loads of nutrients and fiber and keep the contents of your lunchbox interesting. When my grandmother first mentioned her love for a cheese and beetroot sandwich, I was not sure how to feel. I loved beets and cheese, but something about putting them together seemed a little out there. This was yet another tasty bite that surprised me, and adding in more vegetables made me like it even more. Having a lunch filled with color will boost your nutrition, as fruits and vegetables provide different amounts of nutrients important for health, and this sandwich is a great place to start!

INGREDIENTS

Two pieces of whole grain bread, English muffin, or pita
1 tbsp hummus
handful of spinach
¼ cup shredded carrot
2-3 slices of cooked beets about ¼ inch thick*
1 oz of reduced-fat cheddar cheese

DIRECTIONS

Toast 2 pieces of your bread of choice in a toaster or a small pan on the stove with some olive oil or cooking spray.

Spread hummus on the toast to your liking.

Rinse and dry your spinach and place it on top of the hummus.

Rinse the carrot and use a peeler or grater to make carrot shavings and place them on the spinach.

Put your sliced beets and cheese on top and close the sandwich with the other piece of toast.

Slice if desired and enjoy!

PREPARING BEETS

Remove the greens and place whole beets in a pot with the skin still on. Cover with 1-2 inches of water and bring to a boil.

Once they begin to boil, cover the beets and reduce to a simmer and cook until fork tender. This will likely take around 40 minutes but may vary depending on the size.

Drain the hot water and place the beets in a bowl of cold water or add some cold water directly to the pot. This will make them easier to handle.

When the beets have cooled, remove the skin and slice. This should be very easy if cooked sufficiently.

STORAGE

Best enjoyed right away, but it can be wrapped and packed in a lunchbox with an ice pack or stored in the fridge for 2-3 days.

NOTES

*Although a pretty color, beets stain very easily. Be mindful of what you are wearing and touching when preparing them.

To save time, you can purchase cooked beets or pickled beets! You can also buy carrot shavings...they are usually near the baby carrots!

Other greens you may want to try: arugula, cabbage, Swiss chard, or even beet greens.

You could also add sliced tomato or avocado or adjust the contents of the sandwich to your preferred vegetables or the kinds you have on hand!

MINESTRONE SOUP

TOTAL TIME: 50 MINUTES | SERVINGS: 6

On a cool fall day or a snowy winter evening, enjoying a nice bowl of warm soup always makes me feel good. Soup is a great way to use up vegetables you need to eat and is kind of like the savory version of smoothies in that it is an easy way to pack in a lot of nutrients. While I am a lover of various soups, minestrone is one of my favorites. I always get excited to see it on menus and make it at home with my family to cope with New England winters. Whether you are a soup lover or not, I encourage you to explore soup recipes like the one below as they are delicious and nutritious while also being a convenient food to make ahead and a way to reduce food waste!

INGREDIENTS

1 white or yellow onion
3 cloves of garlic
2 large carrots
2 ribs celery
1 medium zucchini
1 cup green beans
1 tbsp olive oil
1 tsp dried thyme
1 tsp dried oregano
2 tsp dried basil
2 bay leaves
¾ tsp salt
½ tsp black pepper
1 15-oz can low-sodium or no salt added crushed tomatoes
1 15-oz can low-sodium or no salt added diced tomatoes
4 tbsp tomato paste
1 15-oz can low-sodium or no salt added kidney beans
6 cups of low-sodium or no salt added vegetable broth
4 cups fresh spinach
½ cup whole grain small shell pasta or other of your choice
salt and pepper to taste
parmesan cheese

DIRECTIONS

Remove the peel from the onion, garlic cloves, and carrots. Rinse all vegetables. Drain and rinse kidney beans and set aside.

Dice the onion, carrots, and celery. Mince the garlic and keep it to the side of your cutting board. Chop zucchini into ¼-inch-thick semicircles and green beans into 1-inch pieces.

Drizzle olive oil in a large pot and set it to medium-high heat. Add the onion, carrots, and celery and stir so that they are coated in oil. Cook for a few minutes or until the vegetables are soft. Now add the zucchini and green beans and cook for another 2-3 minutes.

Lower the heat to medium-low and stir in garlic, spices, bay leaves, salt, and pepper and stir until well distributed. Add tomatoes, tomato paste, kidney beans, and vegetable broth. Cover and cook on medium-low for 10-15 minutes.

Stir in spinach and pasta and cook for another 8-10 minutes uncovered until all vegetables are tender and pasta is al dente. Add additional salt and pepper if desired.

Spoon into bowls and top with parmesan cheese.

STORAGE

Store leftover soup in an airtight container for 3-4 days. Reheat on the stove or in the microwave. You can freeze the soup in freezer-safe bags or containers for up to 3 months. I recommend thawing frozen soup in the fridge overnight.

NOTES

I highly recommend freezing some of the soup if you are just making this recipe for yourself because then you have an easy option ready to go for when you do not want to cook. You can always cut the recipe in half too.

Small pastas you may want to use: ditalini, orecchiette, or small elbows.

If you have them on hand or would prefer to use fresh herbs, you can use them instead of dried.

If you do not like these vegetables, use your favorites or whatever you have on hand (about 2 cups). Some other vegetables I would recommend are potatoes, parsnips, peas, yellow squash, chickpeas, and kale.

If you find that you have lost liquid or feel you want more, just add some water. The longer the soup cooks, the more the liquid evaporates, which thickens the soup.

For extra flavor, add the rind of the parmesan cheese to the soup while it cooks!

SHRIMP AND SALSA LETTUCE WRAPS

TOTAL TIME: 20 MINUTES | MAKES 4-6 WRAPS | SERVINGS: 2-3

Looking for a quick lunch recipe you can easily throw together? Try these shrimp wraps for a protein-packed lunch that will make you feel like you are on vacation! Shrimp don't take long to cook and can easily enhance your favorite salad or grain bowl. This recipe is a fun way to spice up lunch and get some fruit and vegetables into your diet. If you prep it ahead, you will just have to assemble it in the morning before you head out the door!

INGREDIENTS

For the shrimp
8 oz of shrimp, peeled and deveined (fresh or frozen)*
juice of 1 lime, about 2 tbsp
½ tsp chili powder
¼ tsp paprika
¼ tsp garlic powder
olive oil

For the salsa
1 cup fresh pineapple (about ½ a whole pineapple)
¼ cup red onion
¼ cup tomato
1 ½ tsp jalapeño
1 tbsp fresh cilantro (leaves only)
salt and pepper to taste

For the wraps
4-6 pieces of romaine or butter lettuce
1 ½-2 cups cooked rice or quinoa
avocado
pineapple salsa
low-sodium beans
Reduced-fat cheese

DIRECTIONS

If using frozen shrimp, you will want to place the desired amount into a bowl or bag with clean hands and leave them in the refrigerator overnight. If you are in a time crunch, place them in a bowl of cold water for 10-20 minutes, or until completely thawed. Be sure to rinse your hands after handling the shrimp.

While the shrimp thaw, prepare the salsa and cook rice or quinoa according to package directions if you do not have any on hand.

To prepare the salsa, chop the pineapple, dice the red onion, tomato, and jalapeño, and add them all to a bowl. Stir in the cilantro, salt, and pepper and set aside.

Remove the water from the bowl with the shrimp and add the spices and half of the lime juice. Stir until well combined.

Heat a pan on medium heat and add a little bit of olive oil. When the air above the pan feels warm, add the shrimp to the pan and cook for about 2-3 minutes per side. The shrimp will turn opaque and a pinkish color as they cook. You do not want any parts of the shrimp to be translucent. When the shrimp are cooked, add the remaining lime juice.

Rinse and dry the lettuce, add some rice, pineapple salsa, and any other toppings you want to use!

STORAGE

Prepared wraps are best eaten right away, as the lettuce will eventually get soggy; although, you can pack them for lunch with an ice pack if you are eating in a few hours. Store cooked shrimp in an airtight container for 3-4 days in the fridge.

NOTES

*I recommend using small or medium-sized shrimp as they tend to be sweeter, more tender, and fit into the wraps better! Do not use hot water for thawing as this will start cooking the shrimp and affect the texture. Leaving them in cold water for a long time can also negatively affect texture. Also, make sure to only take out the amount of shrimp you plan on cooking as one should not refreeze thawed shrimp due to food safety concerns.

A typical serving of shrimp is about 3 ounces, so with this recipe you will make just about 3 servings. The amount of wraps you can make will depend on how much shrimp you want and the size of the lettuce leaves. I recommend romaine or butter lettuce as it tends to be more sturdy and easily stuffed. That said, be careful not to overstuff the wraps, or they will fall apart on you. If necessary, distribute the shrimp across more wraps.

CAULIFLOWER FLATBREADS

TOTAL TIME: 30 MINUTES | SERVINGS: 4-6

When you think of eating pizza or a tasty flatbread, cauliflower probably does not come to mind. Maybe you have tried cauliflower crusts before and found that they tasted bad, or the texture resembled cardboard. You could say my dad went through a cauliflower pizza era, which made for many questions when I would bring leftovers to lunch. People could not believe I was choosing to eat cauliflower but also marveled at how pretty and tasty it looked. Years later, cauliflower is now one of my favorite vegetables. When designing these recipes, I wanted to find a way to get others to like broccoli's sibling because the cauliflower fan club appears to be lacking members.

INGREDIENTS

For the Crust
4 cups of cauliflower florets
1 egg
2 tbsp flaxseed meal
2 cups all purpose flour
1 tsp baking powder
1 tsp baking soda
¼ cup reduced-fat shredded cheese (e.g., Italian blend)
pinch of salt

Toppings
low-sodium tomato sauce, or your favorite pizza sauce
reduced-fat mozzarella cheese*
fresh basil

DIRECTIONS

You can bake the crust in the oven or make smaller rounds by cooking them in a pan. If baking, preheat your oven to 425°F and line a baking sheet with parchment paper.

Steam the cauliflower in a large pot with about 1-2 inches of water in the bottom. Bring it to a boil first on high heat, then cover and lower to medium heat for about 7 minutes.

Drain the water and mash your cauliflower with a fork, whisk, or potato masher. If you don't want any lumps of cauliflower, blend it up in a blender or food processor.

Add the cauliflower to a large bowl, or just add the ingredients to the pot to save time with dishes.

Stir in the egg and flaxseed meal and continue mixing. Then add the flour, baking powder, baking soda, cheese, and salt.

When transferring to the baking sheet, I recommend dividing the batter in half or quarters and making a few crusts so that way you don't have to assemble all of them at once when cooked. This is helpful if you want to make flatbreads with different toppings too!

Spread the batter out so it's about ½ an inch thick and bake for 13 minutes or until firm. You can cook for longer if you want to brown it or don't intend on making a pizza and cooking it again.

Once cooked, add your sauce, cheese, and any other toppings and bake for another 5-7 minutes. Cool and enjoy!

STORAGE

Keep leftovers in an airtight container in the fridge for 3-5 days.

NOTES

*Reduced-fat mozzarella may take longer to melt. I suggest using shredded reduced-fat mozzarella or slices of full-fat mozzarella if you want your flatbread more cheesy like a pizza.

You can also scoop the dough onto a large pan that has been sprayed with oil and flatten it into a rectangular shape. Flip when only the very middle appears to be wet. This method can help them brown, but it may take longer unless you have a large skillet or griddle.

what's for
DINNER

DINNER

CHICKEN & MUSHROOM GNOCCHI W/ PUMPKIN SEED PESTO	52
VEGETARIAN STUFFED PEPPERS	55
BAKED FISH & CHIPS	57
LEMON PEPPER TOFU BOWL	59
PAN SEARED SALMON & COUSCOUS SALAD	61
BBQ CHICKEN & VEGGIE SHEET PAN	63
FISH TACOS	65
TURKEY BOLOGNESE	67
SINGLE SKILLET STEAK AND POTATOES	69
SHRIMP & VEGETABLE SCAMPI	71

At the end of a long day, cooking a homemade meal might be the last thing you want to do. Cooking for just one person can be hard because most recipes make more than one serving, eating alone can be sad and boring, and the process can be quite lengthy if you are doing dishes by hand or without some help. I get it and want to help you enjoy making dinner…at least a little bit more than before.

I know how hard it can be to find a restaurant that takes allergies seriously and can accommodate your food allergies, but it is possible to find places, and having positive dining experiences is a great way to build your food allergy confidence. The COVID-19 pandemic caused me to eat out much less, although it was never something I did very often. As a result, I began to question the safety of restaurants more than ever before.

Staying optimistic and trying to see the good in all situations is something I try to focus on day to day. I personally believe my nut allergy has shaped who I am in a lot of ways, and while I try to not let it define me and what I am capable of, it is part of my identity. In managing my allergies over the years and periods of lockdowns brought about by the pandemic, I have gotten better at cooking and preparing foods, expanded my list of safe brands, and had fun while doing so. I even make dinner for my family when I am home, as it is a great way to practice and seems only right after all the love, care, support, and meals they have provided me with over the years.

My point with all this is to encourage you to try to see the opportunity that comes with making dinner. It is a time to get better at cooking, discover your likes and dislikes, nourish your body, and refuel for whatever lies ahead.

CHICKEN & MUSHROOM GNOCCHI W/ PESTO

TOTAL TIME: 40 MINUTES | SERVINGS: 6

Pesto, a vibrant green sauce often made from fresh basil, olive oil, garlic, and pine nuts, is a component of many dishes and recipes. It's not uncommon for pesto to be made with cashews or walnuts either, so there are many reasons to stay alert when this word comes up in conversation or on a menu!

Despite growing up in an Italian, food-loving family, pesto was something my family stayed away from for most of my life. The word alone was enough to make me anxious, and for so long I accepted that this was a food I may never get to experience. My grandma and dad suggested we try making pesto with pumpkin seeds instead a few years ago, and since then, this meal has become one of my favorites.

I have yet to try nut-free pesto from the grocery store, at school, or restaurants, but when I am at home, this is a recipe I love to make. Sometimes we add spinach to our pesto if we don't have enough basil or want to sneak in more vegetables. Switching up ingredient ratios can give a different thickness, flavor, and texture too, so I encourage you to try some different variations!

INGREDIENTS

For the pesto
2 cups of fresh basil leaves
1 clove of garlic
3-4 tbsp olive oil
2 tbsp parmesan cheese, or 2 pieces about the length of your thumb
¼ cup of unsalted pumpkin seeds
The juice of half a lemon, about 2 tbsp

DIRECTIONS

Add the basil, garlic, and 2 tablespoons of olive oil to a blender (full-sized or nutribullet will do). If you are using a large blender, you can blend everything at once.

Blend for a few seconds until everything starts to break down. Add in the pumpkin seeds, cheese, remaining oil, and lemon juice. Blend again and taste.

Transfer to a bowl or small container for serving or easy storage.

**When the pesto is made, get the water started for the gnocchi by filling a large pot with water and heating it on high. Add a pinch of salt and lower the heat just before it boils.

For the mushrooms
2 tbsp olive oil
2 cloves minced garlic
2 cups of baby bella mushrooms
1 tsp dried parsley
1 tsp dried basil

Slice your mushrooms thinly on a cutting board along with the garlic.

Heat up a small saucepan for a few seconds and add your oil. When the oil is hot, add in the garlic and stir until fragrant.

Add the mushrooms and cook until tender.

Season with parsley and basil and stir.

Keep the mushrooms on low heat and keep an eye on them while preparing the chicken.

For the chicken
1 lb chicken tenderloins
1 tsp garlic powder
2 tsp dried basil
1 tsp dried oregano
2 tbsp olive oil
1 clove minced garlic

Open your chicken tenderloins and use a fork or clean hands to transfer them to a bowl.

Add in the spices and distribute evenly by stirring.

Heat a large pan with the olive oil. Add in the fresh garlic and cook on medium heat for a few seconds. Make sure the garlic does not burn.

Transfer your seasoned chicken tenderloins to the pan and cook them until you can see that most of the edges are cooked through. This will take about 5 minutes.

Flip the tenderloins using tongs or a fork and cook another 5-7 minutes.

Cut through the thickest piece to make sure it is done inside. Cook longer if necessary; otherwise, slice chicken into 1-inch pieces on a clean cutting board after removing from heat. Add the chicken back to the pan and stir in mushrooms and keep warm.

Other
1 lb gnocchi
parmesan cheese if desired

When the chicken is almost done, bring the water back to a boil. Add gnocchi and cook according to instructions, about 2 minutes. The gnocchi will float when they are done.

Strain the water, then add the gnocchi to the pan with chicken and mushrooms if it will fit. Otherwise, add the chicken and mushrooms to the pot with the gnocchi, or serve from separate pans.

Top with your desired amount of pesto and cheese and enjoy!

STORAGE

The pesto will keep in an airtight container for about 4 days. Store the chicken, mushroom, and gnocchi in a sealed bag or airtight container for 3-4 days.

I recommend storing leftover pesto separately from the other ingredients so everything will last longer without going soggy. This is also helpful when sharing with others so people can add their desired amount.

NOTES

If you prefer, you can leave the chicken whole and just combine the mushrooms and gnocchi, which may help save time. You can also keep just everything separate.

If you ever have leftover pesto or make just the pesto from this recipe, I suggest putting it on pizza or the cauliflower flatbreads, adding it to salads, spreading it on toast, or using it as a dip with crackers or vegetables.

VEGETARIAN STUFFED PEPPERS

TOTAL TIME: 50 MINUTES | MAKES 4 PEPPERS | SERVINGS: 4

With minimal prep work, a lot of flavor, and numerous vegetables, this recipe has you covered! Whether you typically make peppers with ground beef or you have never tried them before, I think this plant-powered recipe might soon be added to your starting lineup! I know all these vegetables might be intimidating, and maybe the thought of a meatless meal gives you the ick, but you might just surprise yourself!

INGREDIENTS

4 bell peppers
1 cup of quinoa*
2 cups of water or low-sodium or no salt added stock of your choice
1 15-oz can of low-sodium or no salt added kidney beans**
1 cup of corn***
1 15-oz can low-sodium or no salt added diced tomatoes
1 ½ tsp garlic powder
1 ½ tsp dried cilantro
½ tsp chili powder
1 tsp paprika
salt and pepper to taste
reduced-fat cheese

Additional toppings
fresh cilantro
sliced avocado

DIRECTIONS

Begin by preparing the quinoa in a pot with the water or stock. Cook on high until it reaches a boil and then simmer for about 20 minutes or until the liquid is gone.

Preheat the oven to 425°F and find a 12x12-inch baking dish or one that will fit your peppers.

Next, prepare your peppers by cutting a circle about 1 inch from the stem. Remove the tops and set them aside. Rinse the peppers to remove any seeds and empty the pepper as best you can without making any other holes.

You will want to cook the peppers a little bit before stuffing them so they are not crunchy. This can be done by boiling them for 5-7 minutes or baking them for about 20 minutes. You do not want the peppers to be soft or mushy because they will be baked again and need to retain their shape.

While the peppers and quinoa are cooking, open the cans of beans, corn, and tomatoes. I recommend removing most of the liquid from the cans so that the filling is not soggy. You will also want to rinse and strain the beans.

STORAGE

Keep leftover peppers or filling in an airtight container in the fridge for 4 days.

NOTES

*Rice can be used instead of quinoa.

Check on the peppers, and when they are slightly tender, carefully strain the hot water and place the peppers in your dish. If they are in the oven, they will be done at almost the same time as the quinoa.

When the quinoa is done, add the beans, corn, and tomatoes to the pot and stir. Add in the garlic powder, dried cilantro, chili powder, paprika, salt, and pepper. The heat from the quinoa will help to warm up the other ingredients, which helps to reduce the amount of time in the oven.

Spoon the mixture into each pepper until full. If you have extra filling, add it to the dish and cover with tinfoil.

Bake for 20-30 minutes or until peppers have reached your desired tenderness. When there are about 10 minutes left, remove the foil and sprinkle some cheese onto each pepper.

Remove from the oven, add any other toppings if desired, and serve warm.

**Substitute any beans you have on hand. If you are not vegetarian and want to increase the protein content, you can add ground chicken, turkey, or beef.

***Canned, frozen, or fresh corn can be used. Feel free to swap carrots, celery, or any other vegetables you like. You may want to cook them a bit before adding to the peppers.

If you want, you can cut the peppers in half before stuffing them. Some people find them easier to eat this way; however, leftovers are harder to store.

When following a vegetarian or vegan diet, paying attention to protein is important as few plant-based sources are complete or capable of providing the 9 essential amino acids we must get from food. Animal proteins are complete, but plant-based options are limited to tofu, quinoa, tempeh, and edamame, unless protein pairing is used. Consuming complementary proteins is effective and important because foods have different amino acid profiles and can fill gaps when put together. For example, beans tend to lack methionine, which is found in grains, and other amino acids missing in grains can often be obtained from beans. Pairing beans and legumes with rice or corn and consuming seed butters with whole wheat bread are a few great options.

BAKED FISH & CHIPS

TOTAL TIME: 50 MINUTES | SERVINGS: 4-5

I still remember the disbelief I felt when my British grandmother told me that "chips" in England are in fact french fries and not the potato chips I was snacking on. They call those "crisps." While the fish and potatoes are deep-fried in an authentic recipe, this baked version is better for your health as it uses less oil and additional seeds! If you ever find yourself across the pond, be sure to try this traditional dish, but for now have fun paying healthy homage to my ancestors from England!

INGREDIENTS

For the fish
1 lb haddock loins
2 tbsp whole wheat flour
1 tbsp hemp seeds
2 tsp dried basil
2 tsp dried parsley
1 tsp garlic powder
1 tsp oregano
1 ½ tbsp flaxseed meal
1 large egg
2 tbsp water

For the chips
2 lbs sweet potato (3-4 cups chopped)
2 tbsp olive oil
1 tsp garlic powder
1 tsp paprika
1 tsp dried parsley
salt and pepper to taste

DIRECTIONS

Preheat your oven to 475°F and line two baking trays with parchment paper.

Combine the flour, hemp seeds, basil, parsley, garlic powder, oregano, and flaxseed meal in a shallow bowl and set aside.

Rinse and peel your sweet potatoes. Cut them in half lengthwise, then place the flat side of the potato down on the board and cut ½-inch thick pieces. Depending on the size of your potato, you may want to cut these pieces in half again. Try to keep the pieces the same size so the fries cook evenly.

Put the sweet potatoes in a large bowl and add the olive oil and seasonings. Stir until well combined and transfer to one of the baking sheets. Bake at 475°F for 20 minutes and stir halfway through.

Now, take your fish out of the fridge and cut it into 3x1-inch pieces on a clean cutting board. Preparing the potatoes first is helpful so that you only need to rinse the board, rather than needing to thoroughly wash it or use a different one.

In a small bowl, beat the egg and water together.

Take a piece of fish, dunk it into the egg, and then dip it into the "breadcrumb" mixture so that all the sides are covered. Then, place the coated fish piece on your other baking sheet and repeat with remaining pieces.

Bake the fish at 475°F for 12-15 minutes or until they start to brown. If needed, broil for 2-3 minutes, but keep a close eye on them so they do not burn. Broiling will also help the fries to get crispy.

STORAGE

Keep leftover fish in an airtight container in the fridge for 3-4 days. Sweet potato fries will also last about 4 days in an airtight container in the fridge.

NOTES

Fish and chips are typically made with cod. If you prefer, you can use cod in this recipe.

If you are not crazy about sweet potatoes or don't have any on hand, you can use white or yellow potatoes. The nutrient profile is very similar; although, sweet potatoes have more vitamin A! For extra fiber, leave the skin on, as that is where most of the fiber is!

I recommend reheating fries in the oven or an air fryer so that they are still crispy!

A serving of fish is typically 3-4 oz, so you will get 4-5 servings from this recipe.

LEMON PEPPER TOFU BOWL

TOTAL TIME: 30 MINUTES | SERVINGS: 4

I'm not going to lie, tofu used to freak me out. Its squishy texture and often bland appearance didn't really appeal to me. After learning about plant-based eating and having some flavorful tofu at home, I had a change of heart. I would not say I am a tofu fanatic, but I do enjoy it.

The dietitian I worked with in college once asked me if I wanted lemon pepper on my tofu, to which I responded with a "What is that?" as I had never heard of it. To my disappointment, I learned that it's actually not a seasoning made from a pepper that's been crossed with a lemon. It's actually a seasoning mix of granulated lemon peel and black pepper. Whether you're a tofu expert, lemon pepper lover, or newbie to both, this easy meal might find its way into your rotation out of simplicity alone.

INGREDIENTS

½ cup dry rice, 2 cups cooked*
1 block extra-firm tofu
1 tbsp lemon pepper seasoning
2 cups of broccoli
1-2 tbsp olive oil
salt and pepper to taste

Optional dressing
3 tbsp dijon mustard**
1 tbsp lemon juice
2 tbsp water
2 tsp low-sodium soy sauce

Additional toppings
Green onion, sliced
Sesame seeds

DIRECTIONS

Preheat your oven to 400°F and line a baking sheet with parchment paper.

Bring a pot of water to a boil to prepare your rice. Cook your rice when the water is ready so that it will be done around the same time as the tofu and broccoli.

Cut the tofu into 1-inch cubes and place them in a bowl with lemon pepper seasoning.

Chop up your broccoli into small pieces if using fresh and add to one side of the baking sheet.

Drizzle the oil over the broccoli and add a little salt and pepper. Use a fork to stir the broccoli around so the oil is well distributed.

Add the seasoned tofu pieces to the other side of the pan and spread out the pieces so they cook evenly.

Place the tray in the oven and bake for 20-25 minutes or until both the tofu and broccoli start to get crisp.

Scoop some rice into your bowl and add the tofu and broccoli. Top with green onions, sesame seeds, and the dressing if desired.

To make the dressing, combine all ingredients in a small bowl.

STORAGE

Store leftovers in an airtight container for 4-5 days. If you have extra dressing and want to store it separately, keep it in an airtight container in the fridge and use it within 7 days.

NOTES

*Use brown rice to increase your consumption of whole grains! If you do not have rice, or you would rather use quinoa, farro, or couscous, you can make that swap, but make sure you read the packaging, as the amount of grain and water needed will vary. Cooking time will also be somewhat different.

**I suggest adding a little mustard at a time to see what you like as it is a strong flavor. For a more mild flavor, you can use hummus instead.

While the tofu and broccoli cook, prepare the dressing by combining all ingredients in a small bowl. If you want a thicker dressing, I recommend adding in some hummus.

Zucchini, cauliflower, and asparagus are great substitutes if you dislike broccoli or do not have any on hand.

PAN SEARED SALMON W/ COUSCOUS SALAD

TOTAL TIME: 30 MINUTES | SERVINGS: 2-3

Salmon provides protein, omega-3 fatty acids, several B vitamins, vitamin D, and minerals such as selenium and phosphorus. This tasty salmon dinner will help you fuel up for tomorrow's adventures and stay on top of your nutrition! Keep an eye on any leftovers...your friends and family might just help themselves.

INGREDIENTS

For the salmon
½ lb filet of salmon (or desired amount)
dried oregano
dried parsley
dried paprika
garlic powder
cooking spray

For the couscous salad
½ cup dry Israeli couscous, ~1 cup cooked*
1 medium carrot, sliced
⅓ cup bell pepper, chopped
1 ⅓ cup Brussels sprouts, quartered
1 cup cherry tomatoes
2 tbsp olive oil
2 cloves of garlic, minced
4 tbsp balsamic vinegar
2 tsp dried oregano
1 tsp dried parsley
1 tbsp honey
salt and pepper to taste

DIRECTIONS

Bring water to a boil to prepare couscous according to the packaging. You will need about ¾ cup water for this much couscous.

While the couscous cooks, chop your vegetables.

Add the olive oil to a small pan on medium heat. Then add the carrots and peppers and sauté for 5-6 minutes.

Once the carrots and peppers are tender, add the Brussels sprouts and cook for another 5 minutes. Toss in the tomatoes when the Brussels sprouts look cooked.

Check the couscous, and if it is done, reduce the heat to low and keep it covered while you finish the vegetables.

Add the minced garlic, balsamic vinegar, spices, salt, and pepper to the vegetables. After 1 or 2 minutes, put it on very low heat while you prepare the salmon.

Carefully skin the salmon with a sharp knife and cut into 3-4-oz pieces if desired.

Coat both sides with your desired amount of spices. I recommend doing a little more than you think you want because some will come off during the cooking process.

Prepare a pan with cooking spray and spray the side of the fish that will be touching the pan to prevent sticking.

Cook on medium-high heat for 4 minutes. Spray the top before flipping and cook another 4 minutes. Continue cooking until golden and crisp.

When the salmon is just about done, add the vegetables to the couscous and mix it all together. You will want to turn the heat up a little so it is nice and hot.

You can cook the salmon a little longer if you want it to have more of a char; otherwise, when it is fully cooked you can serve it up with the couscous salad!

STORAGE

Keep leftover salmon in an airtight container in the fridge for up to 3 days. Store the couscous salad in an airtight container for 5 days in the fridge.

NOTES

*Couscous more than doubles when it is cooked. A serving of cooked couscous is about ½ cup cooked, so this recipe should give you about 2 servings. This can vary depending on the kind of couscous used, so always check out the packaging when preparing it and adjust the amount as needed. If you want additional flavor, you can cook the couscous in a low-sodium broth (e.g., chicken or vegetable broth) instead of water.

When handling fish, always make sure to wash your hands before and after. Wait until the vegetables are cooking before you start handling the fish, or keep the raw fish on a separate cutting board.

The thickness of your salmon filets will determine how long it takes to cook. If you have thicker filets, you may need to cook for about 6 minutes per side.

A serving of salmon is usually 3-4 oz, so the number of servings will vary.

BBQ CHICKEN & VEGGIE SHEET PAN

TOTAL TIME: 35 MINUTES | SERVINGS: ~4

After a long day of class or work, the idea of cooking can seem unbearable and feel overwhelming. Sheet pan meals like this one are a great option because you can cook everything together, which saves time and dishes! Who doesn't love that? If you make the sauce ahead of time, all you need to do is chop and season some veggies, put the sauce on the chicken, and throw it in a preheated oven. So next time you're thinking of DoorDashing or Grubhubbing fast food, think about what's in your kitchen and how you can throw together a quick, healthy meal instead. Your body will thank you!

INGREDIENTS

1 lb chicken tenders
4 small ears of corn
2 small zucchini
½ of a red bell pepper
2 tbsp olive oil
½ tsp oregano
½ tsp garlic powder
salt and pepper to taste
parmesan cheese
dried cilantro

For the BBQ sauce
¼ cup balsamic vinegar
1 tsp garlic powder
½ tsp chili powder
½ tsp paprika
¼ tsp cayenne pepper
2 tbsp tomato paste
1 tsp honey
¼ teaspoon salt

DIRECTIONS

Preheat your oven to 375°F and line a large baking sheet with parchment paper.

Heat a large pot of water on the stove for the corn and bring it to a rolling boil.

Cut the zucchini in half the long way. Then, with the flat surface on the cutting board, slice ¼-inch-thick semicircles and add them to a bowl. Remove any seeds from the bell pepper and cut pieces that are about 1 inch long and ½ an inch wide.

Add peppers to the bowl with zucchini. Season with the olive oil, oregano, garlic powder, salt, and pepper. Stir until well distributed.

Place corn in boiling water and cook for 4 minutes. Carefully drain water when it is done.

Prepare the BBQ sauce in a shallow dish or large bowl by combining the balsamic vinegar with all of the spices, tomato paste, honey, and salt.

With clean hands, open the chicken tenders and place them on one end of the lined baking sheet.

Using a brush or spoon, apply your desired amount of BBQ sauce to the chicken.

You can also place the chicken into the sauce first and coat it that way if you do not have a brush, but it is easy to overdo it when doing it this way. If you want to use any leftover sauce for another dish soon, put some in a container before you start applying it to the chicken, as it will be unsafe to eat once you start dipping the brush back and forth between the chicken and the sauce.

Using tongs or clean hands, place the parboiled corn a few inches away from the chicken in the middle of the baking sheet. Remember the corn may still be hot!

Add your seasoned zucchini and pepper pieces to the other side of the corn.

Finally, spoon a tiny bit of olive oil onto each piece of corn and spin each piece so the corn is coated. Shake some dried cilantro and black pepper on top of each piece and spin them again. If desired, grate some parmesan cheese on top of the corn.

Place the baking sheet into the oven and bake for 20-25 minutes at 375°F. Stir the vegetables and flip the chicken halfway through. Broil for 2-3 minutes if desired.

Cut into your thickest piece of chicken to make sure it's cooked before taking it out of the oven.

Once everything is cooked sufficiently, you are ready to serve!

STORAGE

Keep leftovers in an airtight container in the fridge for up to 4 days. BBQ sauce should be refrigerated and used within 7-14 days.

NOTES

Cauliflower, broccoli, green beans, and asparagus would also work.

FISH TACOS

TOTAL TIME: 25 MINUTES | SERVINGS: 4-5

Tacos of any kind would make my list of favorite foods. They were one of the few foods I could count on in my college dining hall to be safe, and they can easily be personalized to match my mood. If I am out to eat and tacos are an option, there's a good chance I'll be ordering them. Aside from the lobster tacos I had in Rhode Island, few tacos have disappointed me. I think I'd even give the lobster tacos a second chance, as long as they aren't doused in mayonnaise.

While I love many kinds, fish tacos are probably my favorite, despite spending most of my youth thinking fish was gross. If you aren't the biggest fish person or just want to level up your taco game, give these fish tacos a try for a flavorful, protein-packed meal.

INGREDIENTS

½ cup of white onion, sliced
1 Roma tomato, cut into small chunks
2 cloves garlic, minced
1 tsp chili powder
½ tsp paprika
½ tsp garlic powder
¼ tsp cayenne pepper
1 lb fresh haddock or other flaky fish
2 tbsp olive oil
salt and pepper to taste
¼ cup fresh cilantro leaves
8 small tortillas, corn or whole wheat*

Toppings
shredded lettuce
salsa
guacamole (see recipe on p. 110)
reduced-fat cheddar cheese

DIRECTIONS

Cut the onion, tomato, and garlic accordingly on a clean cutting board.

Combine the chili powder, paprika, garlic powder, and cayenne pepper in a bowl.

Unwrap your fish and place it on a different clean cutting board or plate. If it is not already cut, I suggest cutting it into 4-oz pieces as this will make it easier to flip.

Sprinkle both sides of all pieces with the seasoning mixture to your liking. If you prefer, you can shake the seasonings directly onto the fish, but I suggest making the mixture so the flavor is consistent.

If you have any of the spice mixture remaining, add the veggies to the bowl and stir them around until coated, or if the bowl is too small, hold onto it and sprinkle it on top once they are in the pan.

Heat the oil in a large pan and add the onions. Cook on medium-high heat and add the tomatoes and garlic once the onions are fragrant and tender.

After the tomatoes and garlic have been cooking for 2 or 3 minutes, push all the vegetables to the perimeter of the pan and add a little more oil if necessary.

Add the fish to the pan and cook for about 3 minutes a side or until the fish is flaky and no longer translucent. You may want to use some cooking spray on the top of the fish before flipping to prevent sticking.

When the fish is cooked, break up the fish with a spatula and stir it all together. Add any salt, pepper, and cilantro if desired and stir again.

Place the fish on top of warmed tortillas of your choosing. I recommend corn or whole wheat. Add your choice of toppings and dig in! Serve with rice and beans or your preferred side dishes.

STORAGE

Store any extra fish in an airtight container for 3-4 days in the fridge. Keep the fish and toppings separate from the tortillas so they do not get soggy. Heated tortillas are best the same day as they can get chewy in the fridge. Unheated tortillas should be kept sealed at room temperature until the expiration date or for about a month in the fridge.

NOTES

*I suggest corn or whole wheat for both taste and nutrition. Corn and whole wheat options are made from whole grains and have more fiber, so I suggest giving them a try. Always make sure to read the label as ingredients and/or manufacturing can change.

If you want to make extra taco seasoning so you have it ready to use for next time or another dish, set some aside in a bag or avoid touching the fish with a spoon or your hands when going back and forth to the seasoning. This will prevent any bacteria that may be there from getting into the seasoning mixture.

To increase the vegetable content, you could add some bell peppers before the tomatoes or throw some black beans or corn into the pan once the fish is cooked.

Tortillas can be heated in a separate pan with some olive oil while the vegetables and fish cook. You can also wrap them in tinfoil and warm them in the oven.

TURKEY BOLOGNESE

TOTAL TIME: 30 MINUTES | SERVINGS: 4-6

While I never got to meet my great-grandfather from Italy, his love for food and connecting with others over a delicious meal certainly lives on in my family. I have so many fond memories of enjoying spaghetti and meatballs, lasagna, and other Italian dishes at my grandparents' house. Both the nostalgia and complimentary flavors always seem to bring a sense of comfort. Traditional bolognese uses ground beef, pork, or a combination of the two. This recipe uses turkey as it is lower in saturated fat and more heart healthy.

INGREDIENTS

1 large carrot
1 stalk of celery
1 small white onion
3 cloves of garlic, minced
2 tbsp olive oil
1 lb ground turkey
1 cup low-sodium or no salt added chicken stock*
2 cups tomato sauce
1 cup canned diced tomatoes
3 tbsp tomato paste
1 ½ tsp dried basil
1 tsp dried parsley
1 tsp dried oregano
1-2 tbsp fresh basil leaves
1 tbsp pecorino Romano cheese
salt and pepper to taste
1 lb whole wheat or brown rice pasta

DIRECTIONS

Prepare the vegetables by rinsing the carrot and celery, peeling the carrot, and removing the peel from the onion and garlic. At this time you should also fill a large pot with about 4 quarts of water and put it on high heat. Lower the water once it boils as the sauce will need to cook for 15-20 minutes.

Finely chop the carrots, celery, and onion on a cutting board and mince the garlic.

Heat a large pan on medium heat and add two tablespoons of olive oil. When the oil runs, or the pan feels warm when you place your hand above it, add in the carrots and celery. Cook for about 3-5 minutes.

Add in the garlic and the onion and continue cooking for a couple minutes until the vegetables are tender and fragrant.

Create some space in the pan by pushing the vegetables to the edge or one side and add the turkey. Use a spoon or spatula to break up the meat into smaller pieces. Cook the meat for about 5 minutes, or until no pink remains.

Stir in chicken stock, tomato sauce, diced tomatoes, and tomato paste.

Then, add the dried basil, parsley, and oregano. Reduce to a simmer for about 15 minutes.

When the sauce has 10 minutes left, bring the water back to a boil, add a pinch of salt, and the pasta to the pot of water. Cook according to the box instructions. You can leave the salt out at this step, but it will keep the noodles from sticking.

Now add the fresh basil and cheese to the sauce and turn up the heat a little so it is nice and hot. You can add a splash of milk for a creamier sauce. Salt and pepper can be added if desired.

Strain the pasta water and add the pasta to the sauce, or plate the pasta and add your desired amount of sauce.

Top with fresh basil and more cheese.

STORAGE

Keep leftovers in an airtight container or bag in the fridge for up to 4 days, or freezer for up to 3 months.

NOTES

*Turkey or vegetable stock can be used too. I prefer chicken stock and find it more readily available.

The Dietary Guidelines for Americans recommend choosing lean meat, so should you decide to make this recipe with ground beef, aim for 97:3 or 80:20.

You could also utilize low-fat mozzarella or ricotta cheese if you prefer or want to reduce saturated fat more.

SINGLE SKILLET STEAK & POTATOES

TOTAL TIME: 25 MINUTES | SERVINGS: 2-3

During the spring semester of my sophomore year, I went off of my university's meal plan and found myself eating a diet that was limited to packaged snacks, the capabilities of my microwave and mini fridge, and shipments or deliveries of food my dad cooked at home for me. While this was not easy, it was my approach to navigating college life with food allergy anxiety, and I am so thankful for the efforts of my family and allergy-friendly brands.

Getting food from home is something most college students look forward to, but when you've got food allergies and are struggling to navigate life in a new place, it means even more.

Reheating my frozen, home-cooked steak prompted some interesting conversations, as you might imagine, and during these talks it became apparent to me that steak was a food that many people my age missed while at school as it is not something typically found in dining halls. While I understand this is likely due to the expense and valid health concerns about high consumption of red meat, I feel for my friends and wanted to create an easy recipe so they could enjoy a meal that felt home-cooked every once in a while.

INGREDIENTS

1 8 oz sirloin steak
2 cups of baby potatoes
2 cups of asparagus
4 cloves of garlic
2 tsp dried parsley
3-6 tbsp of olive oil
salt and pepper to taste
(about ½ tsp each)

DIRECTIONS

Rinse the potatoes and asparagus and pat dry with a paper towel.

Cut the potatoes in half and place them in a medium-sized bowl. Chop off about an inch from the end of the asparagus (where it is lighter in color). Then cut the asparagus into pieces about 1-inch long and put them in another bowl or push them to one side of the cutting board.

Mince all the garlic and add half to the potatoes along with the parsley. Stir until everything is well distributed.

Heat 2 tablespoons of olive oil in a large pan over medium heat and add the potatoes. Try to make sure the exposed side of the potato is touching the pan as this will help them get crispy. Allow them to cook for about 8-10 minutes.

While the potatoes cook, cut your steak into pieces about 1-2 inches long and season the meat with salt and pepper.

Stir the potatoes and add the asparagus to the pan. Cook for about 8 more minutes. When the veggies are almost done, or cooked to your desired liking, add them to a bowl.

Put two more tablespoons of oil into the pan and add the steak. It will cook fast as the pan has been on, so if you prefer meat that is more pink, lower the heat a little or just watch extra carefully so you do not overcook it. Flip the steak using a fork or tongs so each side browns. Cook about 1-2 minutes per side. Add in the remaining garlic.

When the meat is almost done (barely any pink left), add all the vegetables back to the pan and stir it all around. Cut through the thickest piece of meat to make sure it is cooked enough.

Add more salt and pepper if needed, and you are done.

STORAGE

Store leftovers in an airtight container or bag in the fridge for 3-4 days or in the freezer for 2-3 months.

NOTES

While it is often recommended to prioritize lean proteins (e.g., poultry and fish) or plant-based sources (legumes, seeds, quinoa), red meat is a source of important nutrients. Red meat is a good source of protein, as well as B vitamins and minerals such as selenium, zinc, iron, and phosphorus. When choosing red meat, consider buying sirloin, eye round, top round cuts, or 93/7 or 80/20 ground beef.

Don't be afraid of trying plant-based alternatives either; some of them are quite good!

SHRIMP & VEGETABLE SCAMPI

TOTAL TIME: 20 MINUTES | SERVINGS: 4-6

Shrimp scampi is a favorite food among my college friends. We would always get excited to see it at the dining hall and enjoyed cooking some together over FaceTime during the COVID-19 pandemic. This recipe is perfect for when you're sick of pasta and tomato sauce or are in the mood for something light. With spinach and peas, this recipe has some extra fiber and nutrients, and you don't have to do anything fancy to prepare them.

INGREDIENTS

1 lb of frozen, peeled and deveined Gulf shrimp*
½ fresh shallot, diced
3 cloves of garlic, minced
½ lb thin spaghetti or other pasta**
4 tbsp olive oil
1 tsp dried parsley
1 tsp dried oregano
½ tsp dried basil
½ tsp garlic powder
Juice of one lemon
1 cup low-sodium or no salt added chicken stock
3 cups fresh baby spinach
1 cup frozen peas
1 ½ tbsp of Pecorino Romano cheese
salt and pepper to taste

Optional
¼ cup white wine
1 tsp red pepper flakes
¼ cup fresh parsley

DIRECTIONS

While it is best to put frozen shrimp in a bowl or bag in the refrigerator overnight. You can also put frozen shrimp in a bowl of cold water for 10-20 minutes, or until completely thawed if you are in a time crunch. Be sure to rinse your hands before and after handling the shrimp.

Place a large pot of water on the stove for the pasta and bring it to a boil. While it is heating up, you can gather the other ingredients and get out a large pan.

On a clean cutting board, dice the shallot and mince the garlic.

When the water boils, start cooking your pasta.

Add 2 tbsp of olive oil to the large pan and set it to medium heat. After about a minute, add the diced shallot and garlic. Cook 3-4 minutes or until fragrant.

Drain the water from the shrimp and add the parsley, oregano, basil, and garlic powder to the bowl and stir.

Transfer the shrimp to the pan and cook until pink. About 2-3 minutes on medium-high. Flip as needed to ensure they are cooked.

When the shrimp are done, add the lemon juice and chicken stock and stir. At this point you can add the wine if you are using it.

Next, add in your spinach and peas. They will both cook quickly, so wait until the pasta is just about done. If you cannot fit the vegetables in the pan, you can remove the shrimp and add them back in later.

Strain the water from your pasta and add it to the pan if there's room after reducing heat to low. If your pan isn't big enough, you can add the contents of the pan to the pasta pot or another bowl.

Mix everything together and stir in the cheese. Add salt and pepper if desired.

Top with red pepper flakes or fresh parsley if you want and enjoy.

STORAGE

Store leftovers in an airtight container or bag in the fridge for 3-4 days or in a freezer-safe container for up to 3 months.

NOTES

*I recommend using small or medium-sized shrimp as they tend to be sweeter and more tender. Do not use hot water when thawing the shrimp as this will start cooking the shrimp and affect the texture. Leaving them in cold water for a long time can also negatively affect texture. Make sure to thaw the amount of shrimp you plan on cooking as one should not refreeze thawed shrimp due to food safety concerns.

If you have fresh shrimp, you can use that too, but I suggest buying frozen because fresh shrimp needs to be used right away, and frozen shrimp often tastes better.

A typical serving of shrimp is about 3 ounces. This recipe will give you 4 large servings or 6 smaller ones, so cut the recipe in half or freeze extra scampi if needed.

**It's a good idea to use whole wheat or brown rice pasta to increase your consumption of whole grains. Fiber is more abundant in whole grains, and these varieties may be higher in minerals too. There are also pastas made from legumes like chickpeas you could try for some extra protein. If you want a heartier bite, I suggest using a thicker noodle like linguine.

This recipe is also great with cherry tomatoes and artichoke hearts in addition to or instead of spinach and peas.

time for a
SNACK

SNACK

SUNFLOWER BUTTER ENERGY BALLS	75
YOGURT BARK	76
HUMMUS AND VEGGIES	77
PUMPKIN MUFFINS	78
SEED & DATE POWER BARS	80
HOMEMADE KALE CHIPS	82
CHILI LIME CHICKPEAS	83
FROZEN BANANA BITES	84
BETTER 4 U POPCORN	86
HARD-BOILED EGGS	87

Finding safe snacks has felt challenging at different times, but thankfully it has become a bit easier as more and more nut-free and allergy-aware brands are showing up for those of us with food allergies and dietary restrictions. Even with this progress, however, we are still more limited as these snacks are often not in grocery stores and shops at the airport. Safe packaged items are not always available in cafeterias, breakrooms, or the vending machine in the basement of your dorm or apartment building. Access to these convenience foods appears to be increasing, but there are certainly still times when making and bringing your own snacks is needed, especially as ordering and shipping these specialty snacks is not cheap.

So, let's get snacking! Making your own snacks is fun, nutritious, safe, and delicious! You might just find your friends asking you for recipes or your brother stealing your protein balls, so be prepared and make extras. You might also find your own food preferences changing too and a new sense of creativity.

SUNFLOWER BUTTER ENERGY BALLS

TOTAL TIME: 10 MINUTES | MAKES ABOUT 15 1-INCH BALLS | SERVINGS: 5

Finding nut-free energy bites or protein balls is so tricky at grocery stores. I have found a couple over the years, but I wanted to try making my own so that they would be more interesting and similar to the healthy homemade ones I'd seen online and at local markets. There are so many flavor options and ways to customize energy balls when making them at home, but this simple option never disappoints.

INGREDIENTS

- 1 medium banana
- 1½ cups of rolled oats
- 3 tbsp sunflower seed butter
- 1 tsp cinnamon
- 3-4 tbsp dark chocolate chips

STORAGE

Place the balls into a container and store in the fridge for 4-5 days.

NOTES

To increase the protein and fiber content, add some seeds! I suggest hemp, chia, flax, or pumpkin seeds!

DIRECTIONS

In a medium-sized bowl, mash your banana with a fork.

Add in the rolled oats and stir.

Gradually add in the sunflower butter and stir until the mixture starts to stick together.

Stir in the cinnamon and dark chocolate chips.

Roll the mixture into balls that are about 1 inch in diameter.

YOGURT BARK

TOTAL TIME: 3 HOURS | MAKES 12 PIECES | SERVINGS: 6

If you're in the mood for something sweet, yogurt bark is a healthy snack you should try! It's easy to prepare and a more nutritious option than grabbing a packaged snack. This recipe puts a healthy twist on candy bark and is a fun way to switch from a typical fruit and yogurt bowl. Give it a whirl and play around with the toppings!

INGREDIENTS

2 cups nonfat Greek yogurt
1 tsp lemon zest
½ tsp vanilla extract
2 tbsp honey or maple syrup
fresh blueberries
fresh strawberries
unsalted pumpkin seeds

Other Toppings
dried cranberries, raisins, or dates
sliced banana, blackberries, raspberries
oats or nut-free granola
chia, hemp, or flax seeds
mini chocolate chips

STORAGE

Keep in a freezer safe bag or container for up to 3 months.

NOTES

I do not recommend thawing it in the fridge because the yogurt will melt. Eat it straight from the freezer or take it out of the freezer a few minutes before you plan to eat it if it is really solid.

DIRECTIONS

Line a small dish or baking tray with parchment paper.

Add your yogurt to a small bowl and mix in the lemon zest, vanilla extract, and sweetener.

Transfer the yogurt onto your prepared tray and spread it out across the paper using a knife. I recommend spreading it out until the yogurt is about ¼ inch thick.

Top your yogurt with the berries and pumpkin seeds and place the tray in the freezer until it is completely frozen or for about 2-3 hours.

When it is completely frozen, carefully break the bark into smaller pieces with a sharp knife.

HUMMUS AND VEGGIES

TOTAL TIME: 10 MINUTES | MAKES 1 CUP HUMMUS | SERVINGS: 8 (2-TBSP)

Eating enough vegetables can be tricky if there are few you like or you do not enjoy the cooking process. While I hope this book helps you find many ways to enjoy vegetables and cooking, here's a quick recipe to help you get those veggies in!

INGREDIENTS

1 15-oz can of low-sodium or no salt added chickpeas*
Juice of 1 lemon, about 3 tbsp
2 tbsp of liquid from the chickpeas
2 tbsp olive oil
1 clove of garlic or ¼ tsp garlic powder
½ tsp salt
¼ tahini (optional)**
vegetables of your choice

DIRECTIONS

Strain the liquid from the can of chickpeas into a small bowl. Fun fact: this liquid is called aquafaba.

Rinse your chickpeas and add them to a blender.

Juice your lemon into a small bowl so that any seeds can be easily removed and they do not end up in your hummus!

Add the lemon juice, olive oil, liquid from the chickpeas, garlic, and salt to your blender and blend until smooth. If using tahini, add it in and blend again.

Serve with your favorite vegetables, crackers, or pita, or enjoy on a sandwich!

STORAGE

Store in an airtight container in the fridge for 7 days.

NOTES

*White beans can be substituted for those with a chickpea allergy.

**Tahini is made from sesame, so leave this out if you are allergic or want to share with a sesame-free friend! If you want to replace it, use 1 tbsp sunflower butter for a nutty flavor.

Add some extra nutrients or colorful pizzazz with 1 beet, 1.5 sweet potatoes, or 2 cups of carrots...just make sure to boil, roast, or bake these beforehand and remove the skin!

PUMPKIN MUFFINS

TOTAL TIME: 25 MINUTES | MAKES 12 MUFFINS | SERVINGS: 12

Every year I look forward to fall weather and baking some tasty treats with my family. One of our favorites is muffins, specifically pumpkin muffins; although, we dabble with banana chocolate chip, zucchini, and blueberry varieties too. My dad has made muffins since I was a little girl and recalls me picking out the nuts before I was diagnosed with food allergies. I guess that was my own body protecting me? Over many years, we've tried quite a few recipes and found baking to be a fun way to enjoy a treat that most people can just grab at a coffee shop or their local grocery store. The recipe below is a more nutritious take on pumpkin muffins. Happy muffin making!

INGREDIENTS

1 ¼ cup whole wheat flour
½ cup rolled oats
½ tsp cloves
½ tsp nutmeg
2 tsp cinnamon
¼ tsp ginger
1 tsp baking powder
¼ cup hemp seeds
½ tsp salt
¾ cup milk*
2 large eggs
1 15-oz can pumpkin puree, ~2 cups
½ cup olive oil
½ cup maple syrup
1 tsp vanilla extract

Optional
1 cup raisins or dark chocolate chips
turbinado sugar or seeds for topping

DIRECTIONS

Preheat your oven to 425°F and prepare a muffin tin with liners or baking spray.

Combine the flour, oats, cloves, nutmeg, cinnamon, ginger, baking powder, hemp seeds, and salt in a medium-sized bowl. Set aside.

In a large bowl, whisk together the milk, eggs, pumpkin, oil, maple syrup, and vanilla extract.

Gradually add the dry ingredients to the wet ingredients and stir in between until everything is well combined.

Stir in raisins or chocolate chips if desired.

Fill up each muffin cup to the top.

Add some extra seeds or turbinado sugar to the top if you want additional crunch or sweetness, or just for presentation.

Bake at 425°F for 5 minutes, then lower to 350°F for 16 minutes or until a knife comes out clean.

Allow the muffins to cool for about 10-15 minutes before eating.

STORAGE

Store in a plastic bag or airtight container at room temperature for a week, or freeze them for up to 3 months. If freezing, you will want to thaw them overnight in the refrigerator, then heat them up in the microwave.

NOTES

*I use skim or reduced-fat milk, but you can use your preferred kind. Other nut-free options include fortified soy, hemp, or flax milk, or oat milk! Soy, hemp, and flax milks have added nutrients when fortified and contain more protein, so I suggest them over oat milk. The protein in milk also helps give baked goods structure, which is another reason to choose one with more protein.

If you do not have muffin liners or want to be more sustainable, spray your muffin pan well with a baking spray instead of using butter. I suggest using one made from olive or avocado oil as they contain unsaturated fats that are beneficial for heart health.

SEED & DATE POWER BARS

TOTAL TIME: 30 MINUTES | MAKES 12 BARS | SERVINGS: 12

Finding a granola bar without peanuts and tree nuts is like trying to find a needle in a haystack. If it doesn't have tree nuts, it has peanuts. If it doesn't have peanuts, it's got tree nuts. Even on the occasion that one looks safe, it probably has a warning for cross-contact.

In recent years, more and more allergy-friendly bars have entered the snack market, and some of them are quite good. However, these bars are often affected by the "food allergy tax," which can get expensive. The other tricky thing is that many stores do not carry these allergy-friendly brands.

Because of these various factors, I set out to create a bar I could make at home that would serve the purpose of a granola bar and provide me with energy for class, work, or the gym, and pack some nutrients in too.

INGREDIENTS

5 medjool dates
1 cup rolled oats
¾ cup uncooked quinoa, tricolor or white
⅓ cup honey or maple syrup
1½ tsp vanilla extract
1½ tbsp any seeds, I use hemp
½ cup seed butter*
⅓ cup dark chocolate chips, melted

DIRECTIONS

Preheat your oven to 350°F and prepare a baking sheet, bread pan, or square pan with parchment paper or baking spray. Paper makes it easier to lift the bars out.

Chop the dates into tiny pieces and use a fork to squish them until they start to get sticky and form a paste.

Then, put them in a medium-sized bowl and add in the oats, quinoa, sweetener, vanilla extract, seeds, and seed butter of your choice.

Combine all ingredients with a fork or spoon until it forms one mixture and sticks together. It should hold together easily and should not be runny or very wet.

Transfer the mixture to your pan and press it into the corners and edges of the pan. If using a baking sheet, try to make a nice rectangle and use one of your hands or a knife as a straight edge while molding the rectangle with the other.

Bake for 20-25 minutes or until the bars start to turn golden brown.

Allow them to cool for an hour and then place them in the fridge to further solidify.

STORAGE

Store in an airtight container or plastic bag at room temperature for 5 days or in the fridge for about 10 days.

NOTES

*I like to use pumpkin seed butter for this recipe, but sunflower seed butter also works.

If you are in a dorm and do not have access to an oven, or just in a rush, you can roll the mixture into balls and refrigerate without baking. The quinoa will be a little bit crunchier, so just keep that in mind. They will last 4-5 days in the fridge.

HOMEMADE KALE CHIPS

TOTAL TIME: 30 MINUTES | SERVINGS: ~4

If you are a fan of crunchy snacks or want to add more vegetables to your life, kale chips might just be your new best friend. They have a crunch similar to the potato chips you love but are packed with more vitamins and minerals than potatoes. Making chips at home also gives you the ability to control the amount of salt and fat being added, so you can enjoy a tasty snack that is more heart healthy!

INGREDIENTS

1 bunch of kale
2 tbsp olive or avocado oil
¼ tsp salt

DIRECTIONS

Preheat your oven to 350°F and line a baking sheet with parchment paper.

Rinse your kale and strip the leaves off of it. If they start to break, do not worry as you will be chopping them up anyway.

Chop the kale into small chip-sized pieces and add to a bowl.

Add the olive oil and salt, and stir until the kale is evenly coated.

Transfer the kale to the baking sheet and spread it out a bit so you have 1 even layer.

Bake in the oven for 20-25 minutes.

STORAGE

Keep in an airtight container for 2-3 days at room temperature.

NOTES

Extra seasonings can be added if desired. I suggest garlic powder, chili powder, or nutritional yeast if you want some more flavor or you are not crazy about kale.

CHILI LIME CHICKPEAS

TOTAL TIME: 25 MINUTES | SERVINGS: 4

Finding snacks with protein can be tricky when you can't eat the various bars and trail mixes on grocery store shelves. Chickpeas are a good source of protein and can be a fun snack when roasted, especially if you're sick of eating hummus! You can also add them to salads or wraps too to keep your food interesting!

INGREDIENTS

1 15-oz can of low sodium chickpeas
2 tsp olive or avocado oil
1 tbsp lime zest, ~1 lime*
2 tbsp lime juice, ~1 lime
1 tsp of chili powder
salt and pepper to taste

DIRECTIONS

Preheat your oven to 425°F and line a baking sheet with parchment paper.

Drain and rinse your chickpeas and add them to a small bowl.

Add the oil, zest and juice from the lime, chili powder, salt, and pepper.

Stir the chickpeas until they are well coated with the mixture. Place them on your baking sheet and spread them out a bit.

Bake for 20 minutes and stir them around after the first 10 minutes.

STORAGE

Once cooled, transfer chickpeas to an airtight container and store for 4-5 days. They will lose their crispiness the older they get. Heating them in the oven can bring back some of the crispiness.

NOTES

*Zest your lime before you cut it, and roll the lime on your countertop before you cut it to make it easier to get the juice out. If you don't have a zester or cheese grater, use the juice of another half of a lime.

For a sweet alternative, prepare the chickpeas with maple syrup and cinnamon!

FROZEN BANANA BITES

TOTAL TIME: 75 MINUTES | MAKES ~20 BITES | SERVINGS: 5

These banana bites are simple but mighty when it comes to flavor. While I initially swiped past this recipe on Instagram because it used almond butter, I decided to revisit it and make a nut-free version. Let's just say I have no regrets.

Whether it's the middle of the day or late at night, these bites always hit the spot. Sometimes I like to have these before a workout because they're not super heavy and provide some quick-acting carbohydrates. They are also a great treat for studying or movie watching. You might just find yourself grabbing one or two when getting other ingredients out of the freezer like me...even if it's first thing in the morning!

INGREDIENTS

2 bananas
¼ cup sunflower seed butter*
⅓ cup dark chocolate chips (optional)

DIRECTIONS

Line a baking sheet or plate or dish that is freezer safe with parchment paper.

Peel your bananas and slice them into ¼-inch-thick slices.

Spread a thin layer of the sunflower seed butter onto half of the banana slices and top with another slice of banana so you get a bunch of little sandwiches.

Place the assembled sandwiches onto your lined dish or baking sheet and freeze for about 1 hour so the sunflower seed butter hardens. The next step will be quite difficult if they are not frozen enough.

When the sandwiches appear to be sufficiently frozen, melt your chocolate in the microwave using 30-second intervals and stirring in between until there are no lumps.

Remove the banana bites from the freezer and carefully dunk half of each one into the melted chocolate and place them back on the sheet.

Put the chocolate-dipped bites back into the freezer for about 15-20 minutes so that the chocolate will harden.

Enjoy and transfer extra bites to a freezer-safe container or bag.

STORAGE

Keep these bites in the freezer and they can last about 1-2 months.

The longer they are in there, the more likely they are to get icy and even more solid, so you may need to thaw them for a few minutes if enjoying them weeks later.

NOTES

*Another seed butter or soy-based spread can be used in place of sunflower seed butter if necessary!

Keep in mind that the longer the bites are in the freezer, the harder they will become. You may want to move them to the fridge or leave them on the counter for 5 minutes if they seem really solid.

For a cute party treat, you could cover each bite in chocolate completely, add some sprinkles, and insert toothpicks to make little pops.

BETTER 4 U POPCORN

TOTAL TIME: 5-10 MINUTES | SERVINGS: 2

Inspired by my vegan roommate, Abbi, who introduced me to nutritional yeast, and the many microwave popcorn lovers I met at college, this recipe jazzes up a classic snack we know and love. When I first asked Abbi about nutritional yeast, she told me, "It's cheesy! I put it on everything!" which left me intrigued. Upon further investigation, I learned that this cheese-free, cheesy-tasting powder is also high in many B vitamins!

Plain popcorn is an easy snack to have on hand whether you pop it yourself or buy it at the store. To my surprise, I have noticed more packages with nut-related warnings as popcorn flavors have grown more adventurous. While it may be easy to reach for your go-to microwave buttered popcorn or a package of cheesy popcorn goodness that reminds you of your childhood, consider switching it up with this more nutritious recipe! Abbi and I think you will approve.

INGREDIENTS

5 cups popped popcorn*
2 tbsp olive or avocado oil
4-5 tbsp nutritional yeast
½ tsp garlic powder
½ tsp paprika
salt and pepper to taste

DIRECTIONS

Pop your popcorn if needed and add to a large bowl.

Add the olive oil so it is well distributed, and then add the seasonings.

Stir with a spoon or clean hands until the popcorn is well coated. The yeast may stick to the sides or bottom of the bowl, so keep mixing and add more if needed.

Eat right away for the best snacking experience.

STORAGE

You can store the popcorn in a plastic bag or airtight container for about 3 days, but it is best enjoyed right away as it will get chewy over time.

NOTES

You can use popcorn from a bag or pop kernels on the stove according to directions. Mix this popcorn with other safe snacks (e.g., pretzels, cookie pieces, dried fruit, or candy) for a fun snack mix!

HARD-BOILED EGGS

TOTAL TIME: 10-12 MINUTES | MAKES 6-12 EGGS | SERVINGS: 3-6

Packed with protein, B vitamins, and important minerals, hard-boiled eggs are a great nutritious snack! You can make them quickly and take them on the go, which can help support healthy eating when you are busy with life's adventures.

INGREDIENTS

6-12 large eggs

STORAGE

Consume within 5 days and store in an airtight container in the fridge. Peeled eggs should be eaten in 1-2 days.

NOTES

Don't be alarmed if you see a green ring around the yolk. This is due to a chemical reaction between the sulfur in the egg white and the iron in the egg yolk, which produces iron sulfide! While not appetizing, it is harmless!

DIRECTIONS

Place your desired amount of eggs in a pot and cover the eggs with cold water so that there is about 1 inch of water over them.

Bring the water to a boil by placing the pot on high heat.

Once the water begins to boil, cover the pot with a lid and turn off the heat. If you are using an induction stove, keep it on low because you still want some heat, but if you are using a glass cooktop, gas stove, or stove with coils, shut it off.

Let the eggs sit covered in the hot water for 10-12 minutes. Cooking for 10 minutes will result in a yolk that is a very bright yellow and slightly more moist, while those cooked for 12 minutes will have a flakier yolk that is a bit more pale.

After cooking for your desired time, pour out the hot water and add very cold water to the pot to stop the cooking process. This step is very important as it makes for easy peeling later on and keeps them from overcooking, which can produce a green ring around the yolk! Leave them in the water until they are cool to the touch. If you are cooking in a hurry or making several eggs, you may find it easier to cool them in a bowl of water with ice cubes for five minutes.

did someone say

DESSERT

DESSERT

CHOCOLATE SEA SALT PIZOOKIE	91
FABULOUS FRUIT SALAD	93
ZUCCHINI BREAD	94
BLUEBERRY SURPRISE	95
VANISHING BROWNIES	96
CINNAMON ROLLS	97
SUN BUTTER BLOSSOMS	100
CRANBERRY ORANGE BISCOTTI	102
CARROT CAKE	104
LEMON SQUARES	106

As someone with a major sweet tooth, I find that I am most envious of others' abilities to enjoy any dessert when and wherever they want. Declining cake at birthday parties as a child, skipping dessert at restaurants more often than not, rarely being able to enjoy a boring vanilla ice cream, and dodging various nut-containing cookies at Christmastime are experiences that I have gotten familiar with over the past 17 years. I am sure many of you can relate or know someone with dietary restrictions with similar memories. Despite studying nutrition and enjoying healthy foods often, let it be known that I am no stranger to desserts.

I am fortunate that my parents and extended family got me involved in the kitchen as a child so I could learn to enjoy the process of creating food and find ways to make safe desserts. Baking became a way for me to feel more like everyone else, despite the extra work, time commitment, more expensive chocolate, and inevitable cooking disappointments that happen occasionally. Through my baking trials over the years, I have learned a lot and made some of my favorite memories with friends and family. Homemade desserts often taste better simply because of their freshness and one's ability to choose more real ingredients over preservatives and all those other fun things we often cannot pronounce, and I think the hard work and the heart that you put into your creations makes them more enjoyable too!

There is nothing better than finding a bakery or ice cream shop with nut-free options, or even better, one that is dedicated to being entirely free from nuts. They are rare to come across, but when I have found them, I've felt like a little kid in a candy store. Sometimes these safe options appeared while exploring a random city, and other times positive reviews on food allergy apps like Spokin and AllergyEats prompted planned-out visits. Regardless of the journey, visiting these spots feels like striking gold when you have allergies as they offer a sense of freedom and normalcy that is very often unknown.

While I hope you have found some safe spots to indulge in tasty treats, I am here to provide you with some nut-free recipes for those times when you just need something sweet and in case you do all your baking at home. In my time studying nutrition, I have learned that all foods can fit into a healthy diet. Social media and conversations with others who lack a positive relationship with food can make it easy to think that dessert is off the table if you want to live a healthy life. While it is important to listen to nutrition experts' advice of watching consumption of added sugars and refined grains, I think having a healthy diet is one that is sustainable, and by having a dessert after a meal or a cookie with lunch, one can better manage cravings and prevent the development of an all-or-nothing mindset when it comes to sugar.

Balancing your time and the different parts of life is essential. It is often something people struggle with, whether you're trying to figure out what to do with your life or you have been working the same job for years. I think balance is a key part of nutrition too, and by finding ways to not restrict what may already be a limited diet, you open the door to so much more enjoyment in terms of food and life. Not all desserts have to be laden with butter and sugar, and sometimes a piece of fruit and a cup of tea might suffice. That said, there can be room for cookies and cake too, though it is important to have a varied diet that is not simply just sweets. Whether you are a sweets person or you rarely partake, I hope you share these recipes with others and that they can be a way for you and those you love to make some memories. As one of my favorite country songs says, "life is short, make it sweet...."

CHOCOLATE SEA SALT PIZOOKIE

TOTAL TIME: 35 MINUTES | SERVINGS: 8-10

Chocolate chip cookies are a classic dessert. To take this classic treat up a notch, try making a pizookie or cookie skillet and adding some sea salt! A pizookie is essentially a chocolate chip cookie that's the size of a small pizza. You can divide it into pieces like a pie and put ice cream right on top while it's warm. I've never been able to get one at restaurants, so I made this recipe so I could bring the pizookie to my own kitchen. I decided to add sea salt because I love a sweet and salty flavor combo.

INGREDIENTS

½ cup granulated sugar
¾ cup light brown sugar
½ cup unsalted butter, melted
1 tsp salt
1 large egg
1 tsp vanilla extract
1 ¼ cup all purpose flour
½ tsp baking soda
1 cup dark chocolate chips
sea salt flakes*
cooking spray

DIRECTIONS

Whisk together the sugars, melted butter, and salt in a medium bowl.

Add in the egg and vanilla extract and whisk until well combined. The mixture should run off the whisk when you hold the whisk up.

Incorporate the flour and baking soda so the ingredients are evenly combined, but do not overmix.

Stir in chocolate chips so they are well distributed.

Place the bowl in the refrigerator or transfer the dough to wax paper and refrigerate for 30 minutes. Refrigerating the cookie dough helps develop the flavor and improve the texture of the cookie.

Preheat oven to 350°F and spray a cast iron skillet or cake pan with baking spray.

Transfer the dough to your prepared pan and use clean hands to press it out towards the perimeter so it touches the edge.

Bake for 20-25 minutes or until golden brown and a knife comes out clean.

Sprinkle the top of the pizookie with sea salt flakes while it is still warm. Be careful not to do too many because you can easily overdo it.

Let the pizookie to cool for about 10 minutes, slice it up, top it with your favorite ice cream if you want, and enjoy!

STORAGE

Store pieces in an airtight container at room temperature for up to 3 days, in the refrigerator for about 5 days, or in the freezer for up to 3 months.

NOTES

*Go light on the salt; a little goes a long way!

You can put ice cream directly onto the pizookie, but if you are not sharing it with a large group of people or planning to finish it in one go, I would add the ice cream to the slices so you can save the leftovers!

Looking for cookies instead? Roll the chilled dough into 1-inch balls or use a mini ice cream scoop and bake on a baking sheet lined with parchment paper for 10-15 minutes or until edges start to brown.

FABULOUS FRUIT SALAD

TOTAL TIME: 10 MINUTES | SERVINGS: 3

When you are in the mood for something sweet but don't have the time or energy to make something elaborate, fruit salad is a great choice. The Dietary Guidelines for Americans recommend adults have 1½ to 2½ cup equivalents of fruit daily, and making a fruit salad may help you consume more. A ½ cup of dried fruit and 1 cup of 100% fruit juice also count as 1 cup of fruit. Fruit salads are an excellent way to use up the fruit you have on hand and boost your nutrition with vitamins, minerals, antioxidants, and fiber!

INGREDIENTS

½ cup strawberries
½ cup blueberries
½ cup raspberries
½ cup grapes
1 grapefruit*

Optional
mint leaves (about 1 tbsp chopped)
grapefruit juice*

DIRECTIONS

Begin by rinsing the berries, grapes, and mint leaves in a small bowl or strainer.

On a clean cutting board, slice the strawberries and cut the grapes into halves or quarters. Then add them to a medium-sized bowl or container.

To prepare the grapefruit, carefully cut it in half with a sharp knife. Cut around the inside edge of each half and along both sides of the different sections. Pop out the tiny sections and add them to the bowl. If you want, add a few tablespoons of grapefruit juice to the fruit salad, but watch out for the seeds.

Add the blueberries, raspberries, and mint leaves. Stir together and serve immediately.

STORAGE

Store leftovers in an airtight container or covered bowl in the fridge for about 2 days. Fruit salad is best served fresh, but if you want to have it with breakfast or make it ahead of time, you can. If you plan to use bananas, pears, or apples, you may want to add those right before serving as they will brown.

NOTES

*Grapefruit and related citrus (e.g., Seville oranges, tangelos, pomelos) interact with many medications. Swap in a different fruit or use more berries if needed. You may be able to swap in non-bitter orange and orange juice for a similar taste. Check with your healthcare provider or pharmacist to know what you must avoid.

ZUCCHINI BREAD

TOTAL TIME: 65 MINUTES | SERVINGS: 10

Similar to banana bread, zucchini bread has a moist texture and the perfect touch of sweetness. If you dislike cooked zucchini or want to switch things up, make a loaf of zucchini bread! It's a nice dessert when you are not in the mood for cookies or cake, and it's a good snack to have during the week! Making zucchini bread might just become a relaxing new hobby as baking can have a meditative quality.

INGREDIENTS

1 cup shredded zucchini, ~2 small
⅓ cup olive oil
2 large eggs
½ cup honey
½ cup milk*
2 tsp vanilla extract
1 ½ cups whole wheat flour
1 ½ tsp cinnamon
¼ tsp nutmeg
1 ½ tsp baking powder
1 tsp baking soda
¼ tsp salt
cooking spray

Optional
¼ cup mini chocolate chips

DIRECTIONS

Preheat your oven to 350°F and spray a loaf pan with baking spray.

Shred rinsed zucchini using a large grater and press it with a paper towel to remove excess moisture.

Mix together the olive oil, eggs, honey, milk of choice, vanilla extract, and shredded zucchini.

Add in the flour, cinnamon, nutmeg, baking powder, baking soda, and salt. Stir to combine.

Fold in the chocolate chips if using them.

Pour the batter into the loaf pan and top with extra cinnamon or chocolate chips. Bake for 55-60 minutes at 350° F or until a knife comes out clean.

Cool for 15 minutes and enjoy!

STORAGE

Wrap zucchini bread in foil or keep it in an airtight bag at room temperature for 2 days or in the fridge for up to a week.

NOTES

*I use skim or reduced-fat milk. Other nut-free milks with protein will give similar structure and nutrients. For example, you can use fortified soy, hemp, or flax milk.

BLUEBERRY SURPRISE

TOTAL TIME: 35 MINUTES | SERVINGS: 3

This is an easy recipe my dad used to make when I was a kid. It is straightforward, quick, and relatively healthy compared to many other desserts. I am not sure what the surprise is or where the name comes from, but that's what we have always called it!

INGREDIENTS

1 cup graham cracker or cookie crumbs
2 tbsp maple syrup
½ tsp cinnamon
2 tbsp unsalted butter
2 cups blueberries (fresh or frozen)
cooking spray

DIRECTIONS

Preheat the oven to 350°F and prepare a small baking dish with baking spray. I find that a 9"x9" dish works well.

Mix together the crumbs, maple syrup, and cinnamon.

Cut in the butter so that it stays in some small pieces and makes clusters with the crumbs.

Place 1 cup of blueberries in the bottom of the baking dish and cover with half of the crumb mixture on top. Repeat with the remaining blueberries and crumbs.

Bake for 30 minutes.

Serve warm and with a scoop of vanilla ice cream if you like.

STORAGE

Keep leftovers refrigerated in an airtight container for 3-4 days

NOTES

This is a great way to use up your blueberries if they are starting to get soft.

I like to use oatmeal cookie crumbs because they make it feel closer to a blueberry crisp, but use whatever you have on hand that is safe for you.

VANISHING BROWNIES

TOTAL TIME: 40 MINUTES | MAKES 9 BROWNIES | SERVINGS: 9

Despite being a chocoholic, I have passed up many a brownie thanks to my allergies. Fortunately, I could always count on my mom to make them homemade. Now I know we all claim to have the best recipe, or at least a go-to we love and cherish, but consider giving this one a try for a lower-sugar option with added nutrients. This recipe is free of the top 9 allergens and well-loved by many of my friends! There's a reason for the name.

INGREDIENTS

⅔ cup sunflower seed butter*
½ cup unsweetened applesauce
⅓ cup maple syrup
2 tbsp light brown sugar
⅓ cup cocoa powder
½ tsp salt
1 tsp baking soda
¼ cup sorghum flour**
1 tsp vanilla extract
½ cup dark chocolate chips

DIRECTIONS

Preheat the oven to 350°F and line a 9" x 9" baking dish with parchment paper. Make sure there is enough paper on the sides so you can lift the brownies out of the pan later.

Combine the sunflower butter, applesauce, and maple syrup in a medium-sized bowl.

Stir in the brown sugar, cocoa powder, salt, baking soda, sorghum flour, and vanilla extract.

Mix in the chocolate chips.

Pour the batter into the prepared pan and bake for 35-40 minutes or until a knife comes out clean.

Remove the brownies from the oven and let them cool for 10 minutes before slicing.

STORAGE

Store brownies in a bag or wrapped in foil at room temperature for 3 days or in the fridge for a week. Putting brownies in the fridge can help them firm up but may dry them out.

NOTES

*Any kind of sunflower seed butter that is safe for you will work in this recipe, but I recommend using one without added sugar because of the sugar and maple syrup in the recipe.

**Gluten-free oat flour can be substituted, or you can leave it out. If you do not need this recipe to be celiac or wheat allergy friendly, you can substitute whole wheat flour. Flour helps give the brownies some structure, so they will be a little more gooey without it.

CINNAMON ROLLS

TOTAL TIME: 2 HOURS | SERVINGS: 12

It wasn't until a few years ago that I had tasted a true cinnamon roll. As kids, my brother and I would occasionally have the cinnamon roll-style biscuits by Pillsbury (not as good as I remember, by the way), but otherwise, they were yet another thing made in a bakery, aka the land of cross-contact. When a classmate said her favorite memory was eating cinnamon rolls on Christmas morning, I couldn't help but try to create this experience for myself. It was epic.

INGREDIENTS

For the dough
¾ cup milk*
2½ tsp quick-rise yeast
¼ cup granulated sugar
2 eggs
¼ cup unsalted butter, melted
3 cups all purpose flour
¾ tsp salt

For the filling
¼ cup unsalted butter, softened
⅔ cup light brown sugar**
1½ tbsp cinnamon

For the frosting
3 tbsp unsalted butter, softened
4 oz cream cheese, softened
1 tsp vanilla extract
¾-1 cup powdered sugar

DIRECTIONS

Heat the milk in a microwave-safe bowl for 40-60 seconds, or until it is slightly warm, and transfer it to a large mixing bowl.

Add the yeast to the milk along with sugar, eggs, and melted butter. Stir until well combined.

Incorporate the flour and salt so the mixture forms a dough. You may need to use clean hands to get the flour completely mixed in.

Knead the dough for 5-8 minutes or until you get a nice ball. You can use a dough hook on a stand mixer if you have one; otherwise, knead it by hand on a well-floured surface. Use the heel of your palms to push down and out on the dough, then pick up the side furthest from you, fold it back on itself, and spin it 90 degrees. If the dough is getting stuck to the bowl or counter, add a little bit more flour.

Add about 1 tablespoon of olive oil to a bowl and transfer the kneaded dough to it. Cover with plastic wrap and a warm towel and let the dough rise for 1 hour. The dough should double in size. Time to rise may vary due to temperature and humidity, so adjust as needed.

Place the dough on a well-floured surface and use a rolling pin to create a large rectangle that is about ¼ inch thick. It should be close to 9x14 inches.

Combine the brown sugar, butter, and cinnamon in a small bowl and use a knife to spread it over the entire surface so it is evenly distributed.

Begin rolling from the short side and create a tight roll. Place the seam on the surface and cut about an inch off of each end as these pieces will be smaller and not as full of the cinnamon mixture.

With a sharp knife or floss, cut 1-inch-thick rolls. You will get about 9-12 rolls.

Place the rolls in a 9-inch cake pan or other large baking dish that has been prepared with baking spray. Cover the rolls with plastic wrap and a warm towel again and allow the rolls to rise again for another 20-30 minutes.

While the rolls rise, preheat the oven to 350°F. Once done rising, remove the plastic wrap and bake the rolls for 20-25 minutes, or until the edges begin to brown. I recommend underbaking them a little so that they are soft in the middle.

Make the frosting while they bake by combining the butter, cream cheese, vanilla, and powdered sugar in a bowl using an electric mixer until creamy and smooth.

Cool the cinnamon rolls for 10 minutes before frosting.

Serve them immediately for the best cinnamon roll experience! Reheat leftover cinnamon rolls in the microwave for about 30 seconds.

STORAGE

Keep cinnamon rolls in an airtight container or the baking dish with foil on top for 3 days at room temp or 7 days in the fridge. You can also freeze them for up to 3 months.

NOTES

*I use skim or reduced-fat milk, but you can try this recipe with your preferred kind. Other nut-free options include fortified soy, hemp, or flax milk, or oat milk! Soy, hemp, and flax milks have added nutrients when fortified and contain more protein, so I suggest them over oat milk. The protein in milk also helps give baked goods structure, which is another reason to choose one with more protein.

**If you only have dark brown sugar, you can use that instead.

You can prepare these the night before and put them in the fridge overnight. Let them come to room temperature for 30-45 minutes in the morning before baking.

SUN BUTTER BLOSSOMS

TOTAL TIME: 30 MINUTES | MAKES ABOUT 30 COOKIES | SERVINGS: 15

Having heard people rave about peanut butter blossoms for years, I often found myself wondering about a nut-free version. While I expected this recipe to be an easy one to modify, I was proven wrong. Although I was impressed with the taste and a big fan after substituting sunflower seed butter into my grandmother's recipe, I was horrified to see that the centers of the cookies were a vibrant green color the next day. After some research, I discovered that this green cookie situation was a shared experience and not my fault. It's the product of a chemical reaction between a compound called chlorogenic acid in sunflower seeds and the leavening agents in the recipe! How fun!

After trying a few variations, I think I have finally got it down. This recipe uses reduced amounts of baking powder and baking soda and includes lemon juice. These changes increase acidity, which helps prevent the reaction that turns the dough green. I have received great feedback on this recipe, and so far, it has not produced any green cookies, so I encourage you to give it a try, especially if you have always been wondering about the peanut butter blossom buzz.

INGREDIENTS

½ cup unsalted butter
½ cup granulated sugar
½ cup light brown sugar
½ cup sunflower seed butter
1 large egg
1 cup all purpose flour
½ cup whole wheat flour
½ tsp baking soda
⅓ tsp baking powder, ~¼ tsp + ⅛ tsp
splash of lemon juice, ~1 tsp
30 chocolate drops, squares, or kisses that are safe for you!*

DIRECTIONS

Preheat your oven to 375°F and line a large baking sheet with parchment paper.

Mix the butter and both sugars with an electric mixer or spoon until creamy. Add in the sunflower seed butter and the egg and continue mixing until smooth.

Stir in the flours, baking soda, baking powder, and lemon juice until well combined.

Add some additional granulated sugar to a small bowl. With clean hands, roll the dough into 1-inch balls. Roll each ball in the sugar.

Place the cookies onto your baking sheet about 2 inches apart.

Bake for 8-10 minutes or until the cookies begin to brown.

Remove cookies from the oven and press 1 chocolate into each cookie while they are still warm.

Transfer cookies to a cooling rack or wait until they have cooled a little bit. Enjoy!

STORAGE

Store in a bag or airtight container for up to 5 days. Baked cookies can be stored in the freezer bag for up to 3 months too.

NOTES

*Use your favorite nut-free chocolate when making these cookies for yourself, and if you are making them for someone else, ask the individual what they like to use. People often have different feelings about shared lines and facilities, which is particularly relevant for chocolate, so it's best to check with them.

When bringing these to a party where there will be other nut-containing cookies, I suggest making a separate plate or container for those with allergies that is labeled and covered. Label both containers so that people do not get them mixed up and know the ingredients.

This dough can also be frozen. Place cookie dough balls on a tray in the freezer until they are not sticky and then transfer to a freezer bag. The dough can be stored in the freezer for 6 months, but make sure you thaw it in the fridge overnight before baking!

CRANBERRY ORANGE BISCOTTI

TOTAL TIME: 35 MINUTES | MAKES ABOUT 15 COOKIES | SERVINGS: 15

Making Christmas cookies is one of my favorite memories with my mom. She wanted to carry on a family tradition and help me to enjoy the holiday season, which can be difficult at times when you have food allergies. We modified several family recipes so I could enjoy holiday treats safely and experience the joy of sharing with others. It was not until college that I wanted to try making nut-free biscotti—my brother's favorite. Perhaps it was my youthful aversion to dried fruit or fixation on marshmallows that kept me from making nut-free biscotti when I was younger. Anyway, I have done it now and suggest you try them too!

INGREDIENTS

1¼ cups all-purpose flour
½ tsp baking powder
¼ tsp salt
½ tsp cinnamon
½ cup unsalted butter, room temperature
½ cup granulated sugar
2 large eggs, room temperature
1 tsp vanilla extract
1 cup dried cranberries
1 tbsp orange zest, ~1 orange
3-4 tbsp orange juice, ~1 orange
⅓ cup white chocolate chips

DIRECTIONS

Line a large baking sheet with parchment paper and preheat your oven to 350°F.

In a medium-sized bowl, combine the flour, baking powder, salt, and cinnamon. Then, set the bowl aside for later.

Cream the butter and sugar together until light and fluffy using an electric mixer or spoon if you do not have a mixer.

Reduce the speed a little bit and add the eggs one at a time. Then, add the vanilla and beat for one more minute.

Gradually add in the flour mixture a little at a time on low speed until well combined.

Mix in the orange zest and juice. Stir in the cranberries so they are well distributed.

With clean hands, separate the dough in half and transfer it to a baking sheet. Create a log that is about 8x4 inches and ½-inch thick. You may want to flour your hands to make this easier! For smaller biscotti, split the mixture in half and make two logs that are more narrow.

Bake for 25-30 minutes or until the edges become golden brown. Remove from the oven and allow them to cool for about 10 minutes.

Once they've cooled a bit, slice the log on a diagonal so you make pieces that are about ¾-inch wide. Then, flip each piece so it is flat and bake for another 10-15 minutes.

Remove the biscotti from the oven and allow them to cool.

While they cool, melt the white chocolate for the drizzle. Add the white chocolate chips to a microwave-safe bowl and microwave in 30-second intervals, stirring in between until smooth. You can also use a double boiler if you do not have a microwave by placing the chocolate in a heatproof bowl over a simmering pot of water and stirring until smooth.

Drizzle the chocolate over the biscotti, or dip the end, whichever you prefer! Place them back on the baking sheet so the melted chocolate goes on the parchment paper. The white chocolate will harden as it cools, but to speed this up, you can put the cookies in the fridge!

STORAGE

Keep biscotti in an airtight container or bag for up to 2 weeks.

NOTES

If you do not have dried cranberries, use fresh or frozen instead! I recommend adding them to a pot of boiling water or pouring hot water over them so they pop. Then, spread them on a lined baking sheet and bake at 350°F for 10 minutes. This works best if you do it the night before and leave the cranberries in the oven overnight once it is turned off. The dough may turn a light pinkish color if you go this route. You might consider adding a little bit of sugar, as these cranberries are often a bit more tart than dried varieties.

Baking soda can be used instead if needed, as the orange juice's acidity will activate it.

CARROT CAKE

TOTAL TIME: 60 MINUTES | SERVINGS: 9

My whole life I have heard family members, friends, and others rave about carrot cake and how it is one of their favorite desserts. As a kid, I thought *Ew. Why are these people excited about a dessert with carrots? Crunchy nuts and raisins? Yuck.* As I got older, I grew a bit more curious about this dessert. I mean, how can you not be enticed by cream cheese frosting? Most of the time carrot cake is bad news for those with nut allergies as it usually contains pecans or walnuts. Even if it does not contain nuts, it's usually made in a bakery where cross-contact is a serious risk.

Fortunately, my grandmother used her great baking skills and words of encouragement to get me to try a homemade, nut-free carrot cake when I was in middle school. To this day it remains one of my favorite desserts. It can be weird welcoming a food that you have rightfully ruled as a threat, but baking from scratch in a clean space can expand your list of safe foods and help you feel like you are not missing out. So even if you are a veggie hater, give carrot cake a chance. You probably won't regret it.

INGREDIENTS

For the cake
1 ½ cups shredded carrot
1 ½ cups whole wheat flour
1 ½ tsp baking powder
½ tsp baking soda
¼ tsp salt
1 ½ tsp cinnamon
¼ tsp nutmeg
2 large eggs
½ cup maple syrup or honey
¼ cup olive oil
½ cup milk*
2 tsp vanilla extract
¼ cup raisins
Baking spray

DIRECTIONS

Preheat your oven to 350°F and prepare a 9x9 inch baking dish with baking spray.

Rinse and peel your carrots. Then, shred them using a grater onto a plate. Set aside.

In a large bowl combine the flour, baking powder, baking soda, salt, cinnamon, and nutmeg.

Beat the eggs with a whisk in another large bowl. Whisk in the maple syrup, oil, milk, and vanilla extract.

Gradually add the mixed dry ingredients to the wet ingredients. Once combined, stir in the carrots and raisins.

Use a spatula to transfer the batter to the baking dish.

Bake for 35-45 minutes at 350°F or until a knife comes out clean.

For the frosting
4 oz light cream cheese, softened
½ cup nonfat Greek yogurt
1 tsp vanilla extract
¼ cup powdered sugar

While the cake bakes, prepare the frosting.

Blend the cream cheese in a bowl with an electric mixer.

Once the cream cheese is smooth, add the yogurt and mix again.

Finally, add the vanilla and powdered sugar. Do not overbeat.

Cover the bowl with plastic wrap and refrigerate the frosting until ready to use.

Allow the cake to cool for 10 minutes in the pan. Then move it to a plate or wire rack.

Once the cake is completely cool, spread the frosting on top to your desired thickness.

STORAGE

Store frosted carrot cake in an airtight container in the fridge for 5-7 days. If you have leftover frosting, you can keep it in the fridge in an airtight container for 3 days. I suggest mixing the frosting again before using it.

NOTES

*I use skim or reduced-fat milk, but you can try this recipe with your preferred kind. Other nut-free options include: fortified soy, hemp, or flax milk, or oat milk! Soy, hemp, and flax milks have added nutrients when fortified and contain more protein, so I suggest them over oat milk. The protein in milk also helps give baked goods structure, which is another reason to choose one with more protein.

If you do not like raisins, you can leave them out. For a crunch, you can swap sunflower seeds for the raisins.

You can use a 9-inch round cake pan instead.

If you plan to serve more people, you can double the recipe and use a 9x13 inch pan or two 9 inch pans.

LEMON SQUARES

TOTAL TIME: 50 MINUTES | MAKES ABOUT 9 SQUARES | SERVINGS: 9

If you are not a chocolate-obsessed individual like me or tend to prefer fruity desserts, these lemon squares are the perfect treat for you! They are light, sweet, and tart in the best way possible, and they have a buttery crust at the bottom! These squares are an easy dessert to bring to a party and use ingredients you probably have in your kitchen regularly. Even if you do not think you are a "lemon person," give them a try or at least learn how to make them for your lemon square-loving friends!!

INGREDIENTS

For the crust
6 tbsp unsalted butter
¼ cup powdered sugar
1 cup all purpose flour
2 tbsp cold water

For the filling
2 eggs
¾ cup granulated sugar
4 tbsp lemon juice, about 1½ lemons
1 tbsp lemon zest, about 1 lemon
2 tbsp flour
½ tsp baking powder

DIRECTIONS

Preheat your oven to 350°F and spray a 9x9 inch pan with cooking spray or line it with parchment paper.

Next, blend together the butter and powdered sugar in a mixer or using a hand mixer for about 3 minutes.

Gradually add in the flour, then the water, and continue mixing until dough forms.

With clean hands, squish the dough into a ball and transfer it to the middle of the baking pan.

Spread the mixture around until the bottom of the pan is covered. You can use a glass to roll out any uneven parts and create a smooth crust.

Bake at 350°F for 15 minutes. While the crust is baking, work on the filling.

In a medium-sized bowl with a hand mixer, or using a stand mixer, beat the eggs and sugar together. Then add the lemon juice, lemon zest, flour, and baking powder and mix again until smooth.

Pour the mixture over the baked crust and bake again at 350°F for 30 minutes.

Cool for 15 minutes and dust with powdered sugar once completely cooled.

Cut into squares and enjoy! I suggest cutting it into 9 squares, but if you prefer smaller pieces, you can make 12.

STORAGE

Store in an airtight container or bag in the fridge for 7 days

NOTES

If you are looking to bring these to an event or want to make more, double the recipe and use a 9x13 inch pan or a second 9-inch square pan!

These squares may be paler than you are used to, which is likely due to the reduced amount of sugar because sugar participates in a Maillard reaction with protein, which leads to browning and the development of complex flavors. Although a little lighter in color, this recipe uses about 25% less sugar as many recipes use 1-1½ cups!

just some EXTRA EATS

EXTRA EATS

GUACAMOLE	110
MELON MINT SALAD	111
STRAWBERRY SPINACH SALAD	112
BALSAMIC VINAIGRETTE	113
EASY ITALIAN DRESSING	114
HOMEMADE CHICKEN NOODLE SOUP	115
ROASTED VEGETABLES	117
BAKED POTATOES	119
CHOCOLATE DIPPED ORANGES	121
MUG CAKES	122

In this section you will find an assortment of recipes that did not quite make the cut for a particular mealtime but seemed wrong to omit. You will find dips, salads, condiments, and some other basics that will help you in a pinch or bring a feeling of home and comfort. Whether you are hosting friends for a football game, wishing you had a cup of homemade soup, or simply wanting to expand your skills in the kitchen, this section will help you out! Of course, you can find many of these at the store, and while that is certainly convenient, you might prefer to make your own to save money, improve your nutrition, and reduce stress about cross-contact in the manufacturing process.

In addition, knowing these recipes is valuable as they may help you reduce your food waste. Shopping for one person can be tricky, especially if you are not meal prepping or planning out how you will use what you buy. If you are in the mood for something new or looking to use up the produce you have in your kitchen, consider making one of these recipes!

GUACAMOLE

TOTAL TIME: 10 MINUTES | MAKES 1 CUP | SERVINGS: 2-4

Avocados contain mostly unsaturated fats and provide fiber, which makes them a valuable food for those allergic to nuts! While you can add sliced avocado to toast, wraps, and salads, guacamole makes for an even better avocado-eating experience! Enjoy it for a snack with sliced vegetables, crackers, or chips, or add it to your dinner plate for some extra flavor and color!

INGREDIENTS

1 medium ripe avocado
2 tbsp red onion, diced
¼ cup tomato, diced
¼-½ of a jalapeño, finely chopped
1 tsp minced garlic, ~1 clove*
1½ tbsp lime juice, ~½ a lime
1-2 tbsp fresh cilantro, chopped
⅛ tsp salt

NOTES

I like to add garlic to my guacamole for extra flavor, but it can easily be left out. Customize your guacamole to your preferences and what you have on hand!

DIRECTIONS

Cut the avocado in half on a flat surface and carefully remove the pit. Scoop out the green flesh and mash it in a small bowl.

Add in the red onion, tomato, jalapeño, and garlic.

Juice the lime into a glass or separate bowl to avoid getting seeds in the guacamole. Then, add it to the avocado mixture along with cilantro and salt if desired.

Serve with tortilla chips, vegetables, rice cakes, or use it as a topping!

STORAGE

Guacamole is best enjoyed the same day it's made as exposure to oxygen will cause browning. If you have extra or want to prepare it ahead, put it in an airtight container and press a piece of plastic wrap against the mixture before adding the lid. The guacamole should keep for 3 days this way. Lime juice contains ascorbic acid, which reduces oxidation, so storage time may vary if you skip this ingredient. When you are ready to eat it, you can scrape any discolored guacamole off or just give it a good stir for better color.

MELON MINT SALAD

TOTAL TIME: 10 MINUTES | SERVINGS: 4

This salad is the perfect dish to bring to a summer party and a colorful side to pack in your lunchbox. I remember when I first had this salad at my aunt's house and was easily hooked on it. At first I was a little hesitant to try a salad that was mostly melon and cucumber, but I was hooked from the first bite. I loved the colors and flavors and was soon demanding the recipe. When reviewing the ingredients later on, I was reminded of this recipe's nutritious nature. There's fiber, unsaturated fats, vitamins, minerals, and a touch of protein too.

INGREDIENTS

½ cup olive oil
¼ cup white vinegar
1 tsp salt
¼ tsp ground black pepper
⅛ tsp ground cardamom
½ of a large cantaloupe cut into 1-inch cubes
1 large English cucumber cut into ½-inch semicircles
2 Fresno chiles, sliced thin
¼ cup fresh mint, chopped
¼ cup fresh cilantro, chopped
½ cup unsalted pumpkin seeds

STORAGE

Keep in an airtight container for up to 3 days.

NOTES

Cinnamon or nutmeg can replace cardamom if necessary.

Fun fact: "Pepitas" is Spanish for the seeds of a pumpkin or squash. You might see this term in other recipes or on menus.

DIRECTIONS

In a large bowl, combine the oil, vinegar, salt, pepper, and cardamom.

Add in the cantaloupe, cucumber, and chiles and stir until the dressing has coated everything.

Place in the fridge for about 15 minutes so that the fruits can absorb some of the flavors and to get everything nice and cold.

When you are ready to eat the salad, add in the mint, cilantro, and pumpkin seeds and stir again.

STRAWBERRY SPINACH SALAD

TOTAL TIME: 10 MINUTES | SERVINGS: 2-3

Over the years I have learned that putting fruit in salad can be controversial. Some people get excited about adding pomegranate seeds or orange slices in their salads, while others squirm at the thought of any fruit touching their greens. Because I often found myself passing on the "fun" salads at restaurants, I decided to take matters into my own hands and experiment. I soon realized I'm a fruit-in-salad supporter—it's nutritious, tasty, and it just feels fancy. Check out this recipe to see where you stand!

INGREDIENTS

4 cups baby spinach
1 cup sliced strawberries
½ cup sliced cucumber
¼ of a red onion thinly sliced
2 tbsp hemp seeds

Optional
2 oz feta or goat cheese
1 avocado, sliced

STORAGE

Keep in an airtight container or sealed bag without dressing for up to 5 days. Note that avocado pieces will turn brown and strawberries won't taste as fresh.

DIRECTIONS

Begin by rinsing the spinach, strawberries, and cucumber. Set on a paper towel to dry.

Peel and slice your onion and add it to a bowl while the other produce dries a little.

Slice the strawberries and cucumber and add them to the bowl along with the spinach.

Use a spoon to mix the ingredients and top with the hemp seeds, or another seed you have on hand, and your favorite dressing. I love to top this salad with a balsamic vinaigrette...check out my recipe on the next page!

BALSAMIC VINAIGRETTE

TOTAL TIME: 5 MINUTES | MAKES 1 CUP | SERVINGS: 8 (2-TBSP)

Several years ago a waitress informed me that I could not get the balsamic dressing on my salad. I assumed it was because they ran out. It turns out they had plenty; it just contained walnuts. Ever since that moment, I've been on extra high alert when reading the ingredients of dressings.

Balsamic vinaigrette is one of my favorites. In fact, I used to bring my own to the dining hall because they were usually out, which meant settling for the Italian dressing that was 90% oil. I eventually stopped bringing my own because my container exploded in my backpack, which turned me off from it for a bit. Fortunately, I've rekindled my love for balsamic through learning to make my own, and my backpack no longer smells.

INGREDIENTS

¾ cup olive oil
¼ cup balsamic vinegar
1 tsp Dijon mustard
2 tablespoon maple syrup or honey
¼ tsp garlic powder
salt and pepper to taste (I use ¼ tsp salt, ⅛ tsp pepper)

DIRECTIONS

Mix olive oil and balsamic vinegar in a small bowl with a whisk or a fork so the two liquids combine a little bit.

Add in the Dijon mustard, sweetener, garlic powder, salt, and pepper and mix again.

Enjoy with your favorite salad or any other fun creations!

STORAGE

Place in a small airtight container, mason jar, or bottle and store in the refrigerator for 7 days. One clove of fresh garlic can be used, but note that the dressing will not last as long, and the garlic flavor may become very strong. I recommend using fresh garlic if you plan to use the dressing very soon or serve a lot of people.

NOTES

Salad dressings are often high in fat, sodium, and sugar, and may unexpectedly contain nuts. Some brands may indicate nuts in the name, but it is important to check the label and ask a waiter or chef at a restaurant as nuts can hide in dressings that may sound safe. With this in mind, you may be inclined to explore making your own dressings to use at home or pack for on the go.

When making homemade salad dressing, be mindful of the ingredients you select as dressings with dairy and eggs will not last as long. Adding an emulsifier such as honey, mustard, or maple syrup will provide a thicker texture and help the ingredients mix.

EASY ITALIAN DRESSING

TOTAL TIME: 5 MINUTES | MAKES 1 CUP | SERVINGS: 8 (2-TBSP)

Italian dressing goes on most salads...at least in my world. With olive oil, vinegar, cheese, and some spices from your cabinet, you can easily make this dressing at home. This recipe is easy to make when you run out of your go-to. It can also help you save time and money at the store, so you can spend more time enjoying food and less time reading labels and traveling to various stores.

INGREDIENTS

¾ cup olive oil
¼ cup vinegar (red wine, white, apple cider)
2 tsp lemon juice
1 tsp dried basil
1 tsp dried parsley
1 tsp dried oregano
¼ tsp garlic powder
2 tbsp parmesan cheese
salt and pepper to taste (I use ¼ tsp salt, ⅛ tsp pepper)

DIRECTIONS

Mix olive oil and vinegar in a small bowl with a whisk or fork so the two liquids combine a little bit.

Add in the lemon juice, basil, parsley, oregano, garlic powder, and cheese. Add in any salt and pepper if needed.

Use on your favorite salad or other fun food creations!

STORAGE

Place in a small airtight container, mason jar, or bottle and store in the refrigerator for 7 days. One clove of fresh garlic can be used, but note that the dressing will not last as long, and the garlic flavor may become very strong. I recommend using fresh garlic if you plan to use the dressing very soon or serve a lot of people.

NOTES

Salad dressings are often high in fat, sodium, and sugar, and may unexpectedly contain nuts. Some brands may indicate nuts in the name, but it is important to check the label and ask a waiter or chef at a restaurant as nuts can hide in dressings that may sound safe. With this in mind, you may be inclined to explore making your own dressings to use at home or pack for on the go.

When making homemade salad dressing, be mindful of the ingredients you select as dressings with dairy and eggs will not last as long. Adding an emulsifier such as honey, mustard, or maple syrup will provide a thicker texture and help the ingredients mix.

HOMEMADE CHICKEN NOODLE SOUP

TOTAL TIME: 40 MINUTES | SERVINGS: 6

There's something so comforting about a bowl of chicken noodle soup. Maybe it's the warm broth and noodles, or the nostalgia of eating it at home when I was sick. We all have those foods that remind us of our childhood or favorite place. Chicken noodle soup is one of those foods for me, which is why I wanted to learn how to make it. Keep this recipe in mind for those days when you are feeling under the weather, missing home, or just wanting a nice hot bowl of soup!

INGREDIENTS

2 tbsp olive oil
2 large carrots, ~1 cup chopped
2 stalks of celery, ~1 cup chopped
1 medium white onion, ~1 cup chopped
3 cloves of garlic, minced
8 cups low-sodium or no salt added chicken stock*
2 bay leaves
½ tsp dried oregano
3 sprigs fresh thyme, ½ tsp dried thyme
1 lb skinless chicken breasts, 2 cups if already cooked
¼ cup fresh parsley or 4 tsp dried parsley
salt and pepper to taste
2 cups uncooked egg noodles or pasta of choice
water or more stock if desired

DIRECTIONS

Heat olive oil in a large pot or Dutch oven on medium-high heat.

Add the carrots, celery, and onion. Sauté for 5-7 minutes or until the vegetables start to soften. Add the garlic and stir for another minute.

Stir in the chicken stock, bay leaves, oregano, and thyme. Bring to a boil, then reduce heat to a simmer.

After a few minutes, taste the soup and adjust the seasoning with salt and pepper. You may want to add ½ tsp of salt depending on the stock used and your taste.

Place the chicken breasts into the soup so that the broth covers them. Cover the pot with a lid and cook for about 20 minutes on a low simmer. Stir occasionally.

When the chicken is cooked, transfer it to a plate and add the noodles to the pot. Turn the heat back up so it is boiling. The noodles will take about 6 to 10 minutes to cook depending on the type you use.

Shred the chicken into strips with two forks or cut it into small pieces and add them back to the pot.

Taste the soup and adjust seasoning with more salt and pepper, as needed. Stir in the parsley and serve.

STORAGE

Keep in an airtight container in the fridge for 5-7 days or freeze for up to 6 months!

NOTES

*Bone broth can be used instead of chicken stock.

To save time, you can use a rotisserie chicken or chicken that you have already cooked!

ROASTED VEGETABLES

TOTAL TIME: 20-40 MINUTES | MAKES 2-3 | SERVINGS: 4-6

Roasted vegetables are the perfect side dish or salad topping. Just chop up your favorite kinds, add a little oil, toss them in your favorite seasonings, and throw them in the oven!

INGREDIENTS

Vegetables
asparagus
beets*
broccoli
brussels sprouts
butternut squash
cabbage
carrots*
cauliflower
eggplant
mushrooms
onion
parsnips*
peppers
potatoes (white, yellow, sweet)*
tomatoes
yellow squash
zucchini

Oil
avocado
olive
vegetable

Spices
garlic powder
onion powder
dried oregano
dried parsley
dried basil
lemon pepper
paprika
cumin
cayenne pepper

DIRECTIONS

Preheat your oven to 425°F and line a baking sheet with parchment paper or foil.

Chop your vegetables into 1-inch pieces and add them directly to the baking sheet or to a large bowl.

Drizzle the vegetables with the olive oil and add your desired spices.

Use a spoon to stir the vegetables around on the sheet or in the bowl.

Cook for 15-35 minutes at 425°F. Stir the vegetables halfway through and check on the vegetables periodically to make sure they are not burning.

You can turn the oven up to broil for the last 3-5 minutes if you want, but make sure to watch them as they can easily burn.

STORAGE

Keep roasted vegetables in an airtight container for 3-4 days in the fridge.

NOTES

*Root vegetables will take longer to roast, while cherry tomatoes, peppers, yellow squash, etc. will cook more quickly. Keep this in mind when choosing your vegetables and cutting them.

BAKED POTATOES

TOTAL TIME: 6-60 MINUTES | SERVINGS: 2-4

While this is not much of a recipe, I wanted to include instructions for a baked potato, as potatoes provide micronutrients, such as potassium and vitamins, and they contribute some fiber to your daily intake. They will provide you with carbohydrates needed for a busy lifestyle and are a more budget-friendly option than quinoa, couscous, pasta, etc. If you've got a microwave, making a potato can help save time compared to cooking rice or quinoa if you want something quick after a long day.

INGREDIENTS

2-4 potatoes (any kind)

IN THE MICROWAVE

Poke each potato with a fork in several locations, or use a knife to make a few slits.

Place two potatoes on a paper towel or microwave-safe plate and microwave for 7 minutes per side, or use the 'POTATO' button if your microwave has one.

Use your fork or knife to see if the potatoes are tender. If tender, carefully remove it and allow it to cool for 1 minute. If not, cook in 1-minute increments until desired tenderness is achieved. Repeat with other potatoes. If only making one potato, start with 5 minutes.

IN THE OVEN

Preheat the oven to 400°F.

Poke your potatoes a few times with. a fork, or make slits with a knife, so that steam can exit and the potatoes will not explode.

Place potatoes on a baking sheet or directly on the oven rack if clean. Bake for 30-60 minutes. Time will vary based on the size of the potatoes.

Allow potatoes to cool. Then, cut in half, fluff with a fork, and add any seasonings.

STORAGE

Keep leftover potatoes wrapped in foil or in an airtight container in the fridge for 4 days.

NOTES

Keep an eye on the potato as it cooks in the microwave to prevent overcooking and any microwave incidents. The potato will make some popping and sizzling sounds as it cooks, so don't panic immediately.

Potatoes wrapped in tinfoil can go in the oven but NOT in the microwave. Foil might lead to denser potatoes, but if you are concerned about potential allergens and want to ensure yours is separate and protected, this may be helpful.

If a crispy potato is your goal, I suggest using the oven and spreading some olive oil on the skin. The microwave method is better if you are going for convenience or need a dorm-friendly option.

Add a little salt and pepper or other seasonings to your baked potatoes if you want. You can add any toppings you like, but if you want an alternative to sour cream or butter, I suggest a little olive oil or salad dressing.

CHOCOLATE DIPPED ORANGES

TOTAL TIME: 15 MINUTES | MAKES 10-20 PIECES | SERVINGS: 5-10

You are probably familiar with chocolate-covered strawberries, but did you know you can make a similar treat using oranges? Oranges and other citrus fruits tend to last longer than berries, so buying them may help you reduce food waste! With some sea salt on top, this treat is a nice combo of sweet and salty!

INGREDIENTS

1-2 oranges
¼ -½ cup dark chocolate chips
sea salt flakes

DIRECTIONS

Grab a plastic or paper plate or line a small baking tray with parchment paper.

Peel orange(s) and separate into sections.

Place chocolate chips in a microwave-safe bowl and microwave in 30-second intervals until smooth.

Dip half of each slice into the chocolate and place them all on the tray. Sprinkle with sea salt flakes if desired.

Place the tray in the fridge for 10-15 minutes or until the chocolate is set.

STORAGE

Keep leftovers in the fridge for 3-4 days and keep in mind that the orange will dry out the longer it is in the fridge.

NOTES

I recommend using sumo or navel oranges, but any kind will do! You can also use clementines!

Thinly sliced oranges can be dipped too, but I suggest using the segments to avoid dealing with the peel when eating.

MUG CAKES

TOTAL TIME: 1-2 MINUTES | SERVINGS: 1

Making a traditional cake can be time-consuming and tiring. Despite being a big fan of cakes and cookies (well, most desserts actually), I don't always want to make a full recipe because I am one person. When I was living in a dorm room, I was wishing I knew how to make a dessert in my microwave because that's the only appliance I had. After some research online, I found that mug cakes are easy, single-serve desserts that get pretty close to satisfying a craving for cake. All you need is some standard baking ingredients, measuring spoons, and a microwave, and you are a couple of minutes away from a fluffy, sweet treat.

CHOCOLATE

INGREDIENTS

¼ cup all purpose flour
2 tbsp granulated sugar
½ tsp baking powder
3 tbsp milk*
1 tbsp olive oil
½ tsp vanilla extract

DIRECTIONS

Combine all ingredients in a microwave-safe mug or bowl and microwave for 1.5 minutes. Cool 1 minute and enjoy! Top with powdered sugar, fruit, or whipped cream if desired.

FUNFETTI

INGREDIENTS

¼ cup all-purpose flour
2 tbsp granulated sugar
¼ tsp baking powder
3 tbsp milk*
1 ½ tsp unsweetened applesauce
¼ tsp vanilla extract
1 tsp sprinkles

DIRECTIONS

Combine all ingredients in a microwave-safe mug or bowl. Microwave for 1-1.5 minutes depending on the strength of your microwave. Cool for 1 minute and enjoy! Top with powdered sugar, fruit, or whipped cream if desired.

SB & J

INGREDIENTS

2 tbsp all-purpose flour
¼ tsp baking powder
Pinch of salt
2 tbsp sunflower seed butter
2 tbsp milk*
1 tbsp maple syrup
½ tsp vanilla extract
2 tbsp your favorite jam/jelly

DIRECTIONS

Mix together the flour, baking powder, and salt in a mug or microwave-safe bowl. Add the sunflower seed butter, milk, maple syrup, and vanilla. Stir all ingredients together, then swirl in the jam. Microwave for 1.5-2 minutes depending on the strength of your microwave. Cool for 1 minute and enjoy!

BLUEBERRY MUFFIN

INGREDIENTS

Muffin
¼ cup all-purpose flour
2 tbsp granulated sugar
¼ tsp baking powder
⅛ tsp baking soda
3 tbsp milk*
1 tbsp olive oil
7-10 fresh blueberries

Crumb topping
1 tbsp unsalted butter, chopped
1 ½ tbsp all-purpose flour
2 tbsp brown sugar
⅛ tsp cinnamon

DIRECTIONS

Combine flour, sugar, baking powder, baking soda, milk, and olive oil in a mug or microwave-safe bowl until well combined. Stir in blueberries.

In a separate bowl, combine the ingredients for the topping until the butter is coated in the other ingredients. Add the topping to the mug and microwave for about 1 minute. Cool for 1 minute and enjoy!

NOTES

*I use skim or reduced-fat milk, but you use your preferred kind. Other nut-free options include: fortified soy, hemp, or flax milk, or oat milk! Soy, hemp, and flax milks have added nutrients when fortified and contain more protein, so I suggest them over oat milk. The protein in milk also helps give baked goods structure, so using one with protein will likely make for a better microwave mug cake too.

All microwaves are different, so it may take a few attempts before you figure out what works best for yours. I suggest starting with less time, so it doesn't get too dry.

Mug cakes do not keep well. It is best to eat them right away once slightly cooled.

ADDITIONAL RESOURCES

On my food allergy journey, I have found quite a few helpful resources that may also benefit you or others with food allergies in your life. When I was a child and young teen, many of these resources did not exist and others were just being developed. I was reminded of important allergy management practices and occasionally learned about new research findings through annual allergy appointments, the occasional news story, or class at school, but I have never felt as supported or connected to others with food allergies as I do now, thanks to these resources.

Discovering many of these materials occurred as I battled serious food allergy anxiety for the first time. I remember staying up late searching online to see if anyone had similar experiences and find solutions. While I wish I had the perfect recipe for making allergy anxiety go away, I do not. I have since realized that this funk was probably bound to strike at some point in my life, and I feel grateful I did not have to navigate this at a younger age, though I recognize some kids do. This time has taught me a lot about life and the hardships that others endure whether they have food allergies or not. I have learned that progress is not always linear, self-reflection enables growth, and vulnerability indicates strength and touches others. I realized that fear, anxiety, and depression are common among those in the food allergy community and felt inspired by the stories of others regardless of age.

The food allergy community is so much larger than I ever could have imagined, and thanks to technology, we can now connect with random strangers across the country and world who manage food allergies among other health illnesses and conditions. With many social media platforms, allergy-friendly apps, and food bloggers, we can have that sense of connection and feeling that someone else "gets it" that can be hard to find. How amazing is that? By engaging with others, we can call attention to stories and issues that matter to us, share our favorite safe bites, and be reminded of all the greatness we can achieve.

With that in mind, here are my top five resources for managing food allergies. Check them out on the next page and spread the word—you might just find something that will change your life or save someone else's.

1. https://www.foodallergycounselor.com/
The Food Allergy Counselor, founded by therapist Tamara Hubbard, helps connect people with food allergies to the extra support they need by providing webinars, worksheets, and lists of professionals across the country. When food allergies are the source of stress, anxiety, depression, or trauma in life, it can be easy to say, "It's not that bad," or "It's just food, and I would be silly to see someone about this." Your feelings are not invalid or to be neglected just because you live a different experience. If you have gone through a tough time or you are considering talking to someone, I encourage you to check this page out and explore the available options.

2. https://www.spokin.com/
Spokin is an app where you can leave product and restaurant reviews and find new ones to try. Check out the various guides for traveling, ordering drinks at a bar, and college dining! You will also find a list of verified partners or brands that have participated in an extensive questionnaire about ingredients, labeling, and manufacturing facilities, which makes finding safe snacks and treats easier…and more affordable as they often have discounts and giveaways! Who doesn't want to win nut-free ice cream? (While it might have just been a lucky day, let my win encourage you to enter!)

3. https://www.allergyeats.com/
Allergy Eats is both an app and website that allows you to indicate your food allergies and search for restaurants across the country. You can leave reviews of your dining experiences and use those of others to plan trips or explore the food scene of a new city with additional insight.

4. https://snacksafely.com/
SnackSafely provides snack guides for various food allergies and shares the latest news regarding food allergies. You might find a new snack brand, read about the latest research, or see important warnings regarding food or medical recalls. This website is great for staying in the loop, but know that even tragedies related to food allergies are shared, so spending too much time here might not be beneficial.

5. https://www.foodallergyawareness.org/behavioral-health/faacts-roundtable-podcast/faacts-roundtable-podcast/
On the Food Allergy & Anaphylaxis Connection Team's (FAACT) Roundtable Podcast, you can find interviews and various discussions related to life with food allergies. Managing allergies at school, navigating holidays, talking to family members about preparing food, and understanding school and workplace accommodations are some of the numerous topics covered. FAACT's podcast is available on most streaming platforms.

COOKING TIPS

While the transition to cooking on your own may be intimidating, the more you do it, the more comfortable and confident you will become. Planning out meals, doing your own grocery shopping, and managing your food inventory alone for the first time is difficult, especially if you are a student or navigating a new job.

Below, you will find some words of wisdom for the kitchen that may come in handy or save you from a disaster. Some of these are very general and may seem like common sense, while others are a bit more nuanced. When reading these, you might find yourself thinking *I wasn't born yesterday,* or *Seriously Tori? That's an obvious one!* If that's the case, take what's valuable with you and treat the others as friendly reminders, or at least have a good laugh as you read.

KITCHEN BASICS

1. Use all your senses and have your head on a swivel.

2. Always wash your hands before you cook. This is important regardless of whether you have food allergies and should become a habit.

3. Use separate cutting boards for meats and veggies, or thoroughly wash with dish soap and hot water in between uses if you only have one.

4. Know where that fire extinguisher is and how to use it!

5. Repetition helps with honing your skills and future success.

6. Baking is a science, while cooking is an art. Substitutions and adjustments can significantly impact how your dough rises, pie bakes, or frosting tastes, whereas throwing things together or going off what "looks good" often works fine when cooking.

7. Use that potholder…but not if it's wet. A wet potholder conducts way more heat and will have you dropping some unfortunate words or even your tasty creation.

8. Invest in some decent utensils; the plastic ones break easily, and you will go through them quickly.

9. Keep your fingers away from the blade of the knife when chopping and at an angle so that should a mishap occur, you will hit your nails, not your skin.

10. When cooking fatty meats (sausage, bacon, ground beef, pork, etc.), drain the fat into a separate dish or cup and let it harden. Pouring this liquid down your sink could result in a clogged drain, and pouring hot liquid into the trash may melt the bag and leave you with a nice mess. Some people save fat for other dishes, as it is very flavorful and helpful for browning foods and making sauces. If you are like me, and you are grossed out by the fat, don't feel like you need to keep it!

MICROWAVE MADNESS

1. No metal in the microwave! No metal in the microwave! By the way, no metal in the microwave!

    This means no utensils, foil, packaging, etc. Metal conducts heat, and by placing metal in the microwave, you are setting yourself up for a fire. While I always wondered about the sternness in my dad's voice when it came to this rule and never really believed this safety practice because we can put foil in the oven and use the microwave for short periods of time, my freshman year of college really drove the point home. Just because one foil pouch of onion rings reheated fine doesn't mean the next one won't produce some serious sparks (no, there was not a fire, but you get the point).

2. Foods that are very dry (e.g., a stale brownie or precooked chicken bacon) cook quickly, so stand by and familiarize yourself with how hot your microwave is!

    Trust me, you do not want to be charring a paper towel at 11:30 p.m. or waving pillows and rushing to open windows at 8 a.m., praying to the microwave gods that the fire alarm does not go off.

3. Chocolate burns easily in the microwave! Heat in 30-second intervals and stir after each one to avoid this!

4. Read your plastic wrap boxes, as some of them are not made for the microwave. You do not want any melted plastic in your food.

5. Using a microwave-safe lid or plastic wrap will reduce the time it takes for food to reheat.

FOOD STORAGE

1. Use airtight Tupperware, mason jars, or plastic bags for storing food.

2. Salad leftovers store better without dressing.

3. If something looks bad, smells bad, or tastes bad, it probably is bad. Do not eat it. That said, a banana with brown spots, or a slightly bruised apple is completely fine, so don't be wasteful. If you're unsure, just look it up online.

4. Berries keep best in the fridge and should be rinsed before eating. Putting them on a paper towel will help remove excess water that could make them soggy. Berries can also be rinsed in a 3:1 water-to-vinegar mixture to help extend freshness. It's also best to remove any that are going bad when you first get them.

5. Be careful with the temperature of your fridge. As much as we do not want it to get too hot, we do not want it to be cold either because then food will freeze and unfreeze.

    > I tend to keep my fridge on the borderline too cold setting out of fear of things getting too warm or having a lot cramped into a small space. I'll be the first to tell you, though, that it's better to find the happy medium unless you live for freezing your baby carrots, cucumbers, Greek yogurt, etc., or you are looking forward to scraping ice off the back wall of your mini fridge. Speaking of ice on fridge walls…get rid of it if you can; otherwise, you will have some puddles that further destroy your food. I have had success with a hot paper towel or chiseling away with a plastic knife.

6. Most things get refrigerated after opening. Most condiments are made to be shelf-stable, but stay fresher for longer if kept in the fridge.

7. Putting a piece of plastic wrap over the ends of a bunch of bananas will help delay browning, while putting them in the fridge will speed up the process.

8. If you see one fruit fly, don't let it phase you; he might just be stopping by. If you see a couple, it's time to take action.

    > Add dish soap and apple cider vinegar to a cup or bowl and cover with plastic wrap. Use a toothpick, scissors, or knife to make a few slits. This will allow the flies in but keep most of them stuck. Don't be defeated if you can't see any or don't see any progress after a day or two. They will come. If the cup or bowl is clear, hold it up and look at the bottom…you will be horrified by what you see. Place the trap where the flies seem to be congregating (e.g., near a fruit bowl, or trash can) and be patient.

GROCERY STORE GUIDANCE

Ah, the essential task with which I have a love-hate relationship: buying groceries. When I was a child, grocery shopping was a bit of a drag but sometimes a fun adventure if it involved goofing around with my brother or zooming around with the shopping cart. As I got older and got more interested in nutrition, I liked looking for new brands and helping my parents or family members pick out ingredients for different occasions or school lunches.

Unfortunately, this activity has become slightly less enjoyable and more of a get-in-get-out-as-fast-as-possible type of experience for me. Part of this is because of being a busy, stressed college student, but the main challenge is feeling like I always have to be on high alert as I am a more anxious person when solo. Throw in aisles and shelves of nuts, tables of fresh peanut butter in the middle of the aisle at the front and back of the store (I am talking to you, Big Y), make your own trail mix and nut butters (Hello, Whole Foods), and not to mention the allergy-friendly products are often among the nut-laden health foods. While I know most of these red flags are not as dangerous as they feel, as I am not eating these foods or one with an airborne allergy, it still stresses me out, and I would imagine there are others who feel the same way.

I'm not saying the nonallergic folks should be banned from eating nuts or stores should not sell them, but rather that sometimes it feels like managers of grocery stores, employees, and the general public do not think about how their choices affect others. So, if you feel that too, you are not alone. It is helpful to remember that most of the time nut-containing products are confined to packaging, there are not big clouds of nut dust filling the aisles, you are not being stupid and eating anything risky, and most people do not shop around while eating nuts (with the exception of the rare Karen who insists on enjoying her all-natural, vegan, gluten-free, fair-trade granola while doing her weekly shop).

My point is that grocery shopping is something we need to find a way to feel comfortable doing, even with the mental challenges that it might present. You have probably been in a grocery store over a hundred times. Has there ever been a problem? Do you always bring your epinephrine with you? Have you changed the way you grocery shop? These are questions that I try to ask myself when I get stressed about going. Yeah, I know, a 21-year-old who gets nervous about grocery shopping…It is a little silly, but I know the more I do it, the easier it will get.

On the next page, you will find a range of tips and other things to keep in mind when shopping for your favorite ingredients and other essentials.

1. If you are prescribed epinephrine, bring it with you along with antihistamines just in case. I find that bringing a small backpack, crossbody, or coat or vest with pockets is easiest.

2. Wear a medical ID bracelet or necklace if you have one, and if you do not, consider getting one. As we grow up, we won't always be with someone who knows about our allergies, so this extra precaution can reduce some of the "What if" allergy thoughts and may help in an emergency. I was very hesitant to get one at first as I thought people would ask me about my ugly bracelet all the time or that I would feel like a dog always wearing a collar. The truth is, I rarely notice it, and it gives me confidence when going to class or the gym, and public spaces in general.

3. Have some hand wipes in your car or bag. You can use these to wipe down the handle of your cart or shopping basket if you feel the need, or just for getting rid of germs.

4. Use reusable grocery bags! It's an easy way to help the environment and save money! Leaving them in your car or by your door will help you remember to use them.

5. Go in with a plan! Thinking about what you really need and what you want to spend can prevent you from buying too much or exceeding your budget! I find that writing out a list on paper or in the notes app on my phone is helpful. Writing things down as you run out of them ensures you won't forget when finalizing your list later! I also ask myself the following questions when making my list:

    What do I want to prepare this week?
    What am I almost out of?
    How often do I really eat (insert food item here)?
    Am I cooking for just myself or others?
    Am I travelling soon or going anywhere where I might want to pack food?
    How is the snack supply looking?
    Is there something I want to make and freeze?
    Are there any special brands I need to get from a specific store?
    Do I need to hit multiple stores?
    Am I going to be out and about again soon, or do I want this to last a while?
    Are there any non-food items I need (e.g., sponges, dish soap etc.)?

6. Take a photo of the inside of your fridge or cabinets for reference. This helps you remember what you have as well as see how much space there is for new items.

7. Think about the grocery stores or markets you have access to and compare prices! It might not seem like there is much of a difference, but you will be surprised to see that prices can vary quite a bit!

8. Consider getting a store specific card or becoming a member of your local store's discount program. This can help you get special deals that will add up to valuable savings. These vary by store but may include benefits such as points for gas!

9. Use cash sometimes to help you stick to a budget.

10. Figure out when your store is busiest and shop at off-peak times. People often hit the grocery store on their way home from work, which means 4-6pm is likely a very busy time. Many people also shop during the middle of the day on the weekends for the week ahead. I suggest going early in the morning or checking your stores popular times on Google.

11. Avoid shopping when hungry! You're more inclined to spend with an empty stomach.

12. Inspect your produce before you put it in your basket or cart! Is it unusually soft, smelly, or discolored?

13. Don't buy pre-cut or pre-packaged food if you don't have to. You'll save money by chopping your own onions…even if doing so makes you cry.

14. Know where the nuts are in the store and be aware—people can be messy, and sometimes they might surprise you. Some stores may have stations for making fresh peanut, or nut butters, or dispensers to make customizable trail mix. Allergy-friendly brands are often located in what I call the "Weird Healthy Section" (sometimes called the Natural Foods Section) as it contains quite an interesting assortment of foods. Ironically enough, many nut-free items are stocked in the middle or next to nut-containing products. Reminding yourself that things are sealed, and you aren't actively eating the nut products can be helpful (obviously, there is still risk and should be approached differently for those with airborne allergies).

15. Stick to the brands you know! If it ain't broke, don't fix it. When you are at school and on your own, I suggest using what you know has been safe before vs dabbling in new brands that you might not trust or know much about yet.

16. Download apps like Spokin and Fig to make finding safe brands easier!

17. Read every label, every time! You never know when a company will change a recipe! This goes for foods, drinks, spices, cleaning products, makeup products, hair and body care products, and medications. If you have further questions or cannot find the necessary information (e.g., alcohol is not labeled the same way food is), call or email the company! Nuts can appear anywhere, and you want to stay safe!

18. Consider using self-checkout! It can be intimidating if you have never done it before, but there is usually someone there to assist if you have a question, and it's often faster....even if you have a lot of things. Plus, that way you can bag your items in a way that makes sense for unpacking, which can also help save time.

19. Make the grocery store your last stop! You do not want eggs, milk, meat, frozen items, etc. sitting around in your car for a long time!!

20. Talk to a manager if there is a certain brand or product you want to see in store! They might be able to stock it for you, which could save you money and time if it means you won't have to shop online or visit multiple stores.

21. Ask your friends, family, or roommates if they need anything while you're out. It's a nice thing to do and can help them out if they are busy.

22. Investigate grocery store pick-up options or try out delivery services like Instacart!

ACKNOWLEDGEMENTS

Despite being a passion project and life goal to make meaningful contributions to society, this book was part of my honors thesis and presented an opportunity to learn, which is one of the things I value most in life.

I want to thank Dr. Lisa Troy, who served as the chair of my thesis committee, along with committee members Dr. Sarah Gonzalez-Nahm and Dr. Heather Wemhoener, who supported my project and were an integral part of my academic journey at UMass Amherst.

Thank you to my family members and friends for your continued support and encouragement throughout the project. A special shout-out is in order for my grandmother, Joan, who suggested the title!

To everyone who tasted my recipes and provided feedback, thank you for letting me bombard your taste buds, and I hope you had fun trying them.

Finally, thank you! Yes, you, the reader! Thank you for giving this a read! I hope you learned a thing or two and found some new recipes for yourself or the awesome people in your life who are allergic to peanuts and/or tree nuts!

THE FINAL WORDS

Be safe, have fun, and try new things!
Happy eating!

~Victoria